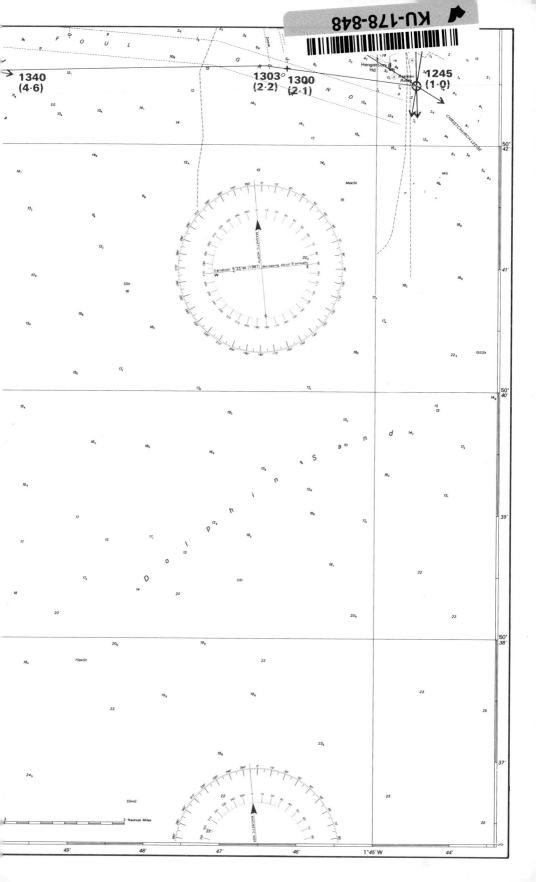

DAY SKIPPER

Pilotage and Navigation

Other books for RYA courses

Competent Crew
An Introduction to the Practice and
Theory of Sailing
Pat Langley-Price and Philip Ouvry
ISBN 0 229 11736 8

For the novice who is totally
unfamiliar with the sea. Subjects are
explained from first principles and a
glossary helps clarify nautical terms.
The book covers the RYA practical
Competent Crew course and much of
the Day Skipper shorebased course.

Yachtmaster
An Examination Handbook with
Exercises
Pat Langley-Price and Philip Ouvry
ISBN 0 229 11662 0

This very popular and widely used
classroom textbook provides a course
manual for the whole of the
shorebased syllabus of the RYA/DTp
Yachtmaster Offshore Certificate, plus
extra material on specialised topics.
There are Test Papers and exercises at
the end of each chapter, all of which
are based on Admiralty Instructional
Chart No 5055. A section of the chart
is printed inside the jacket.

Yachtmaster Exercises
Pat Langley-Price and Philip Ouvry
ISBN 0 229 11715 5

This companion volume to *Yachtmaster*
is packed with practice exercises and
answers, including over 50 model
plots. Use it to polish up before the
exam or in classroom exercises. It
comes complete with a full sized
Admiralty Instructional Chart 5055.

Coastal Navigation 3rd Edition
Gerry Smith
ISBN 0 229 11709 0

This programmed learning book is
designed to teach navigation
(including the navigation syllabus of
the RYA Yachtmaster course) to the
beginner. It is now updated to include
the latest buoyage changes. Admiralty
Instructional Chart 5050 is included.

Ocean Yachtmaster
Celestial Navigation: An Instructional
Handbook with Exercises
Pat Langley-Price and Philip Ouvry
ISBN 0 229 11695 7

The ideal classroom course textbook
for the thousands who embark each
year on the most advanced RYA/DTp
grade – the Yachtmaster Ocean
Certificate. Using this book and its
exercises the student will be able to
study from home.

Ocean Yachtmaster Exercises
Exercises in Celestial Navigation
Pat Langley-Price and Philip Ouvry
ISBN 0 229 11792 9

Companion volume to *Ocean
Yachtmaster* for those taking the
Yachtmaster Ocean Certificate and for
navigators' revision.

VHF Yachtmaster
Pass Your Exam the Easy Way
Pat Langley-Price and Philip Ouvry
ISBN 0 229 11720 1

This textbook and its accompanying
cassette have been produced as a
complete self-tutor for the aspiring
operator who wishes to become a
fluent radio communicator. It
includes all the information necessary
to pass the examination.

DAY SKIPPER

Pilotage and Navigation

PAT LANGLEY-PRICE
and PHILIP OUVRY

ADLARD COLES
8 Grafton Street, London W1

Adlard Coles
William Collins Sons & Co. Ltd
8 Grafton Street, London W1X 2LA

First published in Great Britain by
Adlard Coles 1988

Copyright © Sirius Sailing and Marine Limited 1988

British Library Cataloguing in Publication Data
Langley-Price, Pat
  Day skipper
  1. Seamanship. Navigation—For yachting
  Yachts. Pilotage—Manuals
  I. Title   II. Ouvry, Philip
  623.89'0247971

ISBN 0-229-11829-1

Printed and bound in Great Britain by
Hartnolls Ltd, Bodmin

All rights reserved. No part of this publication may be
reproduced, stored in a retrieval system, or transmitted,
in any form, or by any means, electronic, mechanical,
photocopying, recording or otherwise, without the prior
permission of the publisher.

Contents

List of Plates

Acknowledgements

The authors wish to thank the following: Roger Hunter, Barnacle Marine Ltd for use of Stanford charts; Thos Reed Publications Ltd for use of extracts from Reed's Nautical Almanac; W. & H. China; Philip Klein. Extracts from Admiralty tide tables are reproduced with the sanction of the Hydrographic Department, MOD.

Introduction

'Classroom navigators are all very well,' said the principal of a practical sailing school, 'but they do seem to find it difficult to put theory into practice.' 'Why don't you write about pilotage: taking a boat in and out of harbours and around the coast with plenty of buoys and landmarks,' he continued, 'and while you are about it, explain how to read a chart: to recognise the buoys, beacons, lighthouses, headlands, chimneys, towers, transits, leading lines, clearing bearings and so on. And make it suitable for motor boats as well, not just sailing boats.'

Having completed *Competent Crew*, which is *an introduction to the practice and theory of sailing*, and having written *Yachtmaster*, which is *an examination handbook for students on Royal Yachting Association (RYA) courses*, it seemed appropriate to take up the points made by the sailing school principal with *an introduction to the practice of pilotage and navigation* suitable for the explorer of creeks and estuaries, the local fisherman, the coast hugger, the motor boater and the trailer sailor, the learner, the less experienced . . . This is it: this is *Day Skipper*.

What have we done in *Day Skipper?* We have headed for the quiet backwaters of Poole Harbour and the adjoining coastline from Swanage to Christchurch. Very conveniently Stanfords produce a yachtsman's chart covering the area which includes a wealth of information on pilotage, weather forecasting and emergency procedures. All the exercises are set on this chart and a practice version is enclosed with the book. We have added useful bits of information on different techniques and methods to cover completely the pilotage and navigation syllabus for the RYA Day Skipper qualification. We have included a full description of electronic navigation aids which are becoming inexpensive enough to be installed in many small craft. There are examples and exercises, with illustrations and fully worked answers. We have also included over 25 photographs to show how the symbols and views on the chart appear in practice. For anyone cruising around Poole it is almost a guidebook in itself; but we must not say *guidebook*, it's not nautical: it should be *pilot* or *sailing directions*. Yes, we have included the right nautical terms with a full explanation of their meanings.

It has been hard work to produce and we hope you find it useful. Please let us know, through the publisher, if you have any suggestions or comments.

We do wish you happy sailing; and safe navigation.

Pat Langley-Price
Philip Ouvry

Chapter One

What is a Chart?

A chart is a seafarer's map. It is used like a map to identify: a position; a destination; and the best route between the two.

Fig 1.1 shows a portion of the chart which covers the area from Needles, Isle of Wight, to Start Point. The title is: *The English Channel from the Needles to Start Point* and the chart number is 12. It is a small scale chart showing a large area but not much detail and is used for planning a sea passage. Now look at chart number 15 (provided) which covers the area from Durlston Bay to Christchurch Bay. It is of a larger scale than chart 12 (Fig 1.1) and contains much more detail. This type of chart is used when approaching a harbour or an anchorage as many of the features and hazards shown are omitted on a small scale chart.

Refer to chart 15. The title and number of the chart are shown on the outside cover and repeated on the map side. Under the title there is an explanation of the symbols and abbreviations used together with navigational information. To the left, about half way down, are tables showing the direction and rate of the tidal streams at specific places. The chart is metric which means that all heights and depths are in metres. Distances are always in nautical miles, and speeds or rates are in knots, which are nautical miles per hour.

Fig 1.2 shows a compass rose which is used to define direction. It is graduated in degrees (°) from 0 through 360. There are three compass roses on chart 15.

The latitude scale is down each side of the chart and the longitude scale is along the top and bottom. These scales are used in the same way as a grid on a map to identify a specific position. The latitude scale is also used for measuring distance.

On the reverse side of the chart is navigational and pilotage information.

In the next chapter the chart is explained in detail.

1

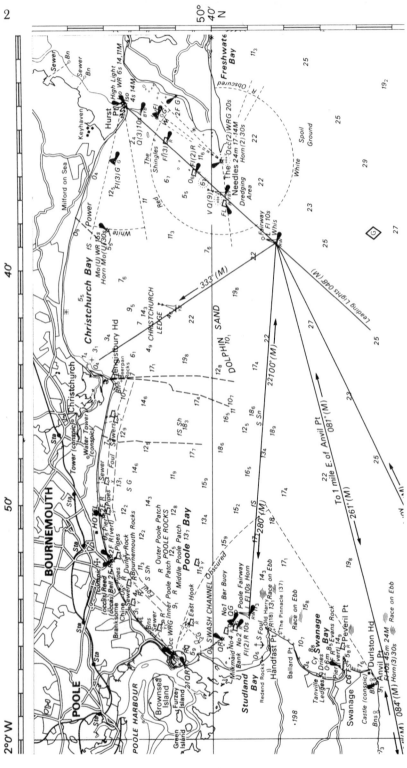

Fig 1.1 A portion of small scale chart 12 English Channel

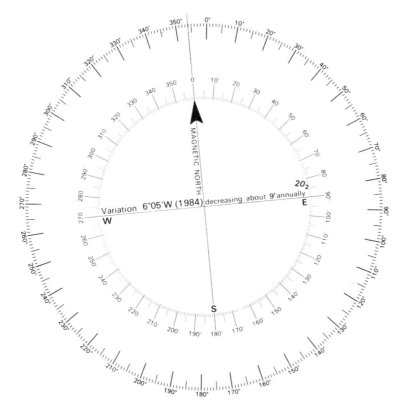

Fig 1.2 A compass rose

QUESTIONS

Use chart 15 to answer these questions.

1.1   What is the main difference between chart 15 and the portion of chart 12, (Fig 1.1)?

1.2   What is the title of chart 15?

1.3   What are the figures:
a. down the side border of the chart;
b. along the top and bottom of the chart?

1.4   How can a specific position be identified on chart 15?

1.5   What is a knot?

Chapter Two

How a Chart is Made

A chart is a representation of a portion of the earth's curved surface projected on to a flat area. There are several ways of doing this but the main type of projection used on navigational charts is called **Mercator**.

Fig 2.1a represents the earth, overlaid with imaginary lines of latitude and longitude. Lines of latitude (known as parallels of latitude) are equally spaced either side of the Equator. Latitude is 0° at the Equator increasing to 90° at each pole. Lines of longitude (known as meridians) converge at the North and South Poles. The meridian passing through Greenwich, London, is the datum meridian for longitude. Longitude is 0° at Greenwich increasing to 180° east and west of the Greenwich meridian.

Fig 2.1b represents a mercator projection chart. Parallels of latitude and meridians of longitude appear as parallel lines at right angles to each other. To allow for the east–west distortion caused by this projection, the parallels of latitude are spaced increasingly further apart as the distance from the Equator increases. On this form of projection a straight line representing the track of a vessel crosses all meridians at the same angle. Such a line is known as a **Rhumb Line**. Because of the distortion of this projection, mercator charts cannot be used either for polar regions (latitudes greater than 70°) or for passages in excess of 600 nautical miles. The charts in these cases use a **Gnomonic** projection which has the advantage that a straight line on the chart represents the shortest distance on the earth's surface. For convenience large scale charts, such as chart 15, use a gnomonic projection; though for navigational purposes they can be used as a mercator projection.

Both latitude and longitude scales are divided into units called degrees (°) with sub-divisions into minutes (') and tenths of a minute. There are 60 minutes in one degree. Sixty degrees ten point five minutes would be written: 60° 10'.5. Like a grid, coordinates from

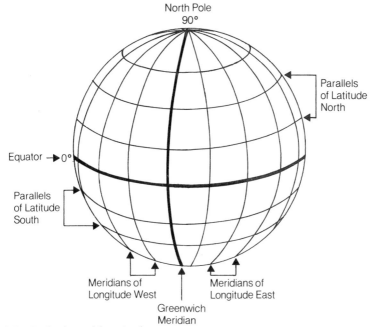

Fig 2.1a Latitude and longitude

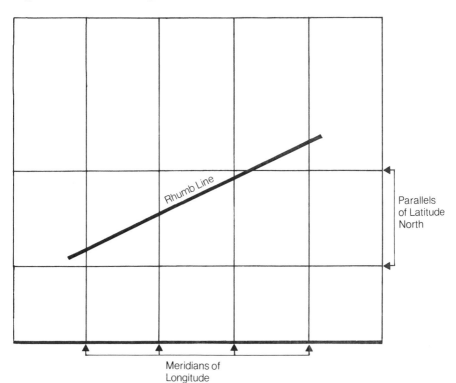

Fig 2.1b Mercator projection

both scales are used to identify a position. The latitude scale is also used for measuring distance because one minute of latitude is equivalent to one nautical mile (M). (A nautical mile – 6076 feet or 1852 metres – is not equal to a statute mile – 5280 feet.) With mercator projection as latitude increases the scale increases, so distance must *always* be measured from the latitude scale level with the boat's position (Fig. 2.2).

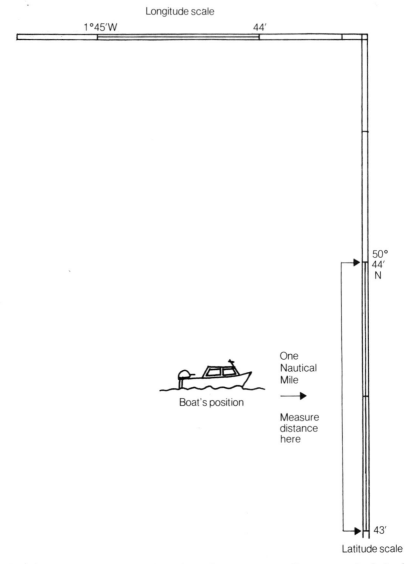

Fig 2.2 Latitude and longitude scales. Always measure distance on the latitude scale level with the boat's position.

QUESTIONS

2.1   Why is it important to measure distance from the latitude scale in the area of the boat's position?

2.2   What are the properties of a mercator projection chart?

2.3   Why is it not possible to use mercator projection charts for polar regions and for passages over 600M?

2.4   What is the datum meridian for longitude?

2.5   How would you write in figures: Fifty degrees, thirty eight point five minutes?

Chapter Three

Using a Chart

Refer to chart 15.

To measure on a chart latitude, longitude, direction and distance
the normal navigational instruments used are a parallel rule and
dividers. These instruments are used in the explanations in this

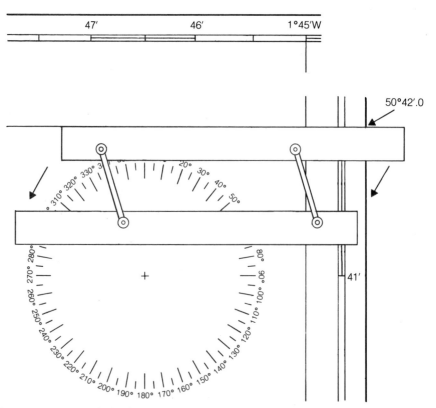

Fig 3.1a Measuring latitude

book. Other navigational instruments (such as Douglas and Portland protractors, Breton and Hurst plotters) are often more convenient on a small boat; and they are supplied with a full set of
instructions.

To measure latitude

Look at the compass rose at the top right-hand corner of the chart.
To find the latitude of the centre point of this compass rose, place
the closed parallel rule along the parallel of latitude nearest to the
compass rose, 50° 42'.0. Keeping a firm hold on the top half of the
rule, move the bottom half until the bevelled edge passes through
the centre point, Fig 3.1a. It will intersect the latitude scale to the
right of the compass rose, Fig 3.1b. The figure on the scale through
which it passes is 50° 41'.0. The latitude of the centre point of the
compass rose is 50° 41'.0N: north (N) because the latitude is north
of the Equator.

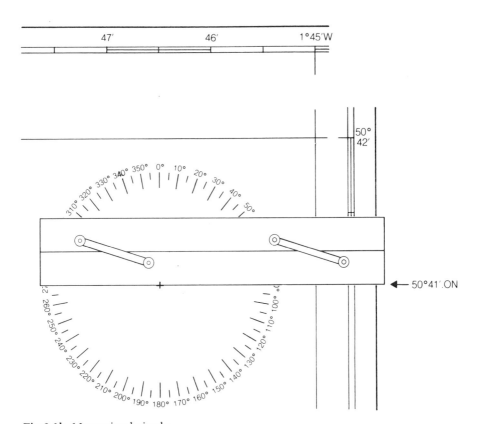

Fig 3.1b Measuring latitude

To measure longitude

To find the longitude of the centre point of the same compass rose, place the closed parallel rule along the meridian of longitude to the right of the compass rose, 1° 45′.0, Fig 3.2a. Move each half of the parallel rule alternately across the chart (known as 'walking' the rule) so that the edge passes through the centre point. It will intersect the longitude scale at 1° 46′.5, Fig 3.2b. The longitude of the centre point of the compass rose is 1° 46′.5W: west (W) because the longitude is west of the Greenwich meridian.

Now use the dividers to do the same exercise. Place one point of the dividers on the meridian to the right of the compass rose (1° 45′W) and the other point at the centre of the compass rose, Fig

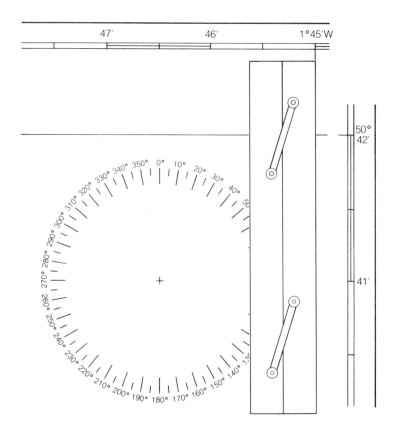

Fig 3.2a Measuring longitude

3.3. Keeping the dividers this distance apart, transfer them to the top longitude scale. One point will be at the intersection of the meridian; the other will be on the figure 1° 46′.5. The longitude at the centre of the compass rose is 1° 46′.5W. So the longitude found by using the dividers corresponds with that found using the parallel rule (Fig 3.2b). Similarly latitude can also be found using dividers. In practice the parallel rule and dividers are used together: one for latitude and the other for longitude.

Recording a position

When recording a position, latitude is written first followed by longitude; 50° 41′.0N 1° 46′.5W.

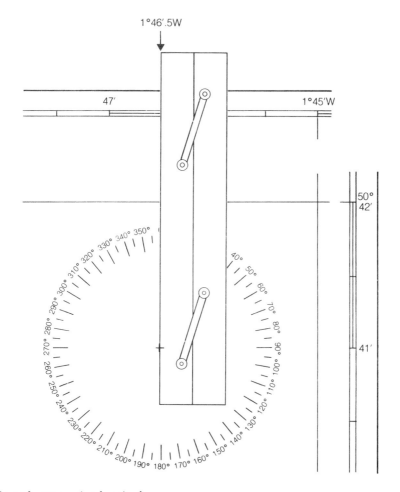

Fig 3.2b Measuring longitude

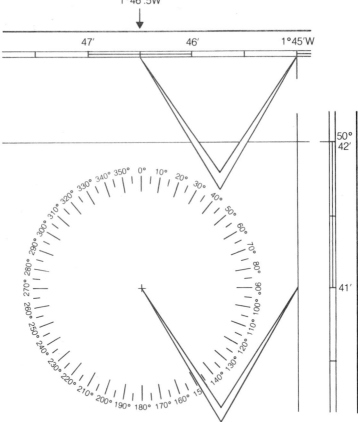

Fig 3.3 Using dividers to measure longitude

Plotting a position

Now plot position 50° 41′.5N 1° 45′.5W. This is the reverse of the previous procedure. Place the parallel rule along the meridian nearest to 1° 45′.5W: this is 1° 45′.0W. Walk it to the right until the edge intersects the longitude scale at 1° 45′.5W. Leave the parallel rule in this position. Use the dividers to mark off the latitude. Place one point on the parallel nearest to 50° 41′.5N: this is 50° 42′.0N. Place the other point on 50° 41′.5N. Keeping the dividers this distance apart, move them to the parallel rule with one point on the parallel 50° 42′.0N. The other point will be on the required latitude of 50° 41′.5N. Mark the position, Fig 3.4.

Finding direction

Examine the compass rose (Fig 1.2). This consists of two circles both graduated through 360°. For the moment we are only concerned

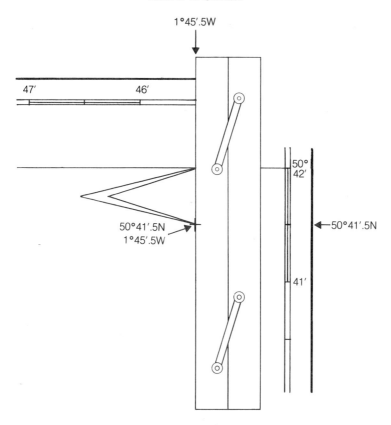

1°45'.5W

47'   46'

50°
42'

50°41'.5N
1°45'.5W

←50°41'.5N

41'

Fig 3.4 Plotting a position

with the outer circle. Place the parallel rule across the compass rose so that the edge passes through the centre and the figures 0° and 180°, Fig 3.5a. The figure 0° represents the direction of geographical north (called true north) and the figure 180° is the direction of south. Direction is measured clockwise from true north through 360°.

Place the parallel rule with its edge across the centre and through the figures 90° and 270°, Fig 3.5b. The rule is now in an east–west direction in line with the parallels of latitude, 90° is east and 270° is west.

Now imagine that you are standing at the centre point of the compass rose looking out in the direction of the figure 40°, Fig 3.6. A line drawn from the figure 40° to your position would, if extended, pass through the figure 220°. The same line can indicate two directions. Walk forward towards the figure 40°: you are now travelling in the direction of 40°. For clarity the directions round the compass rose

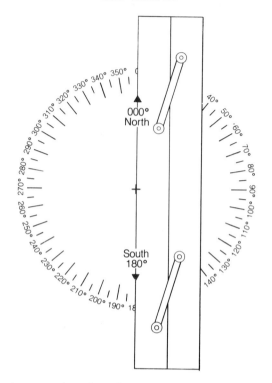

Fig 3.5a Direction – north and south

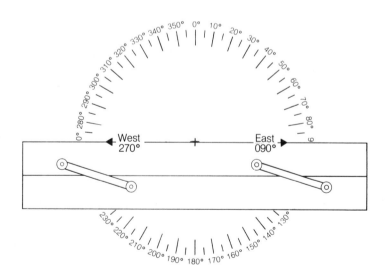

Fig 3.5b Direction – east and west

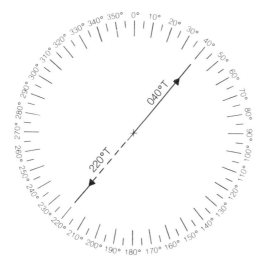

Fig 3.6 Finding direction

are abbreviated. In practice directions are given using a three figure notation, so 40° would be written 040°. We have used true north as our reference point so we can indicate this by putting the letter 'T' after the figures; so 040° becomes 040°T. The direction behind us is known as the reciprocal direction and always differs by 180°: it is 220°T. A boat pointing in the direction of 040°T is on a course (or heading) of 040°T.

Suppose we are in a boat in a position 50° 42′.5N 1° 47′.0W and we wish to find the direction of the beacon at the end of the groyne off Hengistbury Head (50° 42′.6N 1° 44′.9W). Align the edge of the parallel rule between the boat's position and the beacon, Fig 3.7. Walk the parallel rule so that the edge passes through the centre of the nearest compass rose. It will pass through the figures 85° and 265°. The beacon at the end of the groyne off Hengistbury Head from the boat's position is in the direction of 085°T. It is said to be on a bearing of 085°T. From the beacon the bearing of the boat is 265°T, this being the reciprocal of the bearing 085°T. A reciprocal bearing is always 180° different from the original bearing.

If the parallel rule is a Captain Fields pattern engraved with a protractor scale, Plate 1, it is not necessary to walk it across the chart to the compass rose. There is an easier way. For example, from the position 50° 42′.8N 1° 49′.0W, we wish to know the bearing of Boscombe Pier (50° 43′.0N 1° 55′.0W). Place the edge of the parallel rule between our position and Boscombe Pier, Fig 3.8.

Walk the rule to the nearest meridian so that the intersection of the S (south) line and the edge of the rule is *exactly* on the meridian.

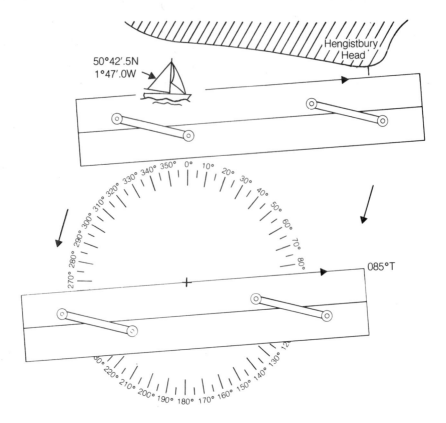

Fig 3.7 Using the compass to find direction

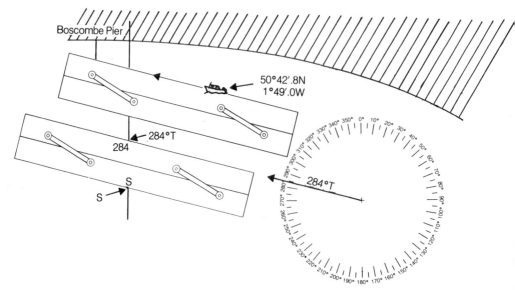

Fig 3.8 Using a parallel rule to find direction

Close the other part of the rule. Follow the meridian up from this point of intersection to the scale and read off the figures. We have two figures one of which is the reciprocal of the other. If you are not sure which is correct, imagine you are at the centre of the compass rose looking outward. In this case the bearing of Boscombe Pier from our position is 284°T.

Wind directions are always given as the direction *from which* the wind is blowing using the compass point notation rather than the 360° notation, Fig 3.9.

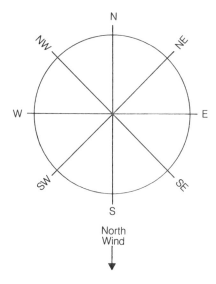

Fig 3.9 A north wind blows *from* the north

Measuring distance

Distance is measured in nautical miles. By definition one nautical mile is equivalent to one minute of latitude. Distance is always measured on the latitude scale level with the area concerned. (On a large scale chart, such as chart 15, there is occasionally a mean distance scale. This is not included on a small scale chart.)

To measure the distance from the centre of the compass rose (50° 41′.0N 1° 46′.5W) to the beacon at the end of the groyne off Hengistbury Head, open out the dividers putting one point on each of the two positions. Keeping the dividers at the same distance apart, transfer them to the latitude scale alongside, Fig 3.10. They span one complete graduation and 0.95 of the next. As one graduation (one minute of latitude) is equivalent to one nautical mile, the distance from the centre of the compass rose to the beacon is 1.95 nautical

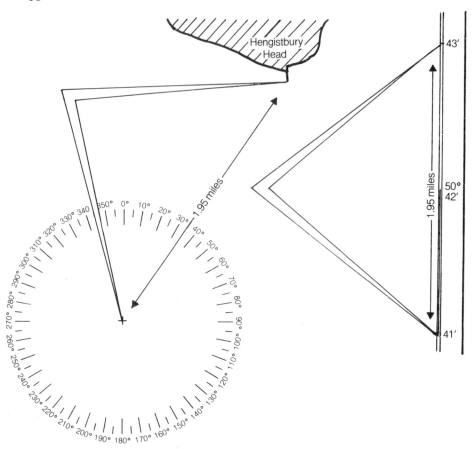

Fig 3.10 Measuring distance

miles (or 1.95M). In practice we only work to the nearest tenth of a nautical mile, so we would write 2.0M.

Now measure the distance between the centres of the compass roses in positions 50° 36'.3N 1° 46'.5W and 50° 40'.0N 1° 53'.1W. The dividers are too small to span this distance. Open the dividers to a convenient distance, say 2.0M, and 'walk' them from one position towards the other, Fig 3.11.

After two spans the distance remaining is less than 2.0M. Set the dividers to this remaining distance and measure it off on the latitude scale: it is 1.6M. The total distance is 5.6M (2.0+2.0+1.6).

To measure a given distance from a position, set the distance on the dividers using the latitude scale (level with the required area) then place one point of the dividers on that position and the other in the given direction.

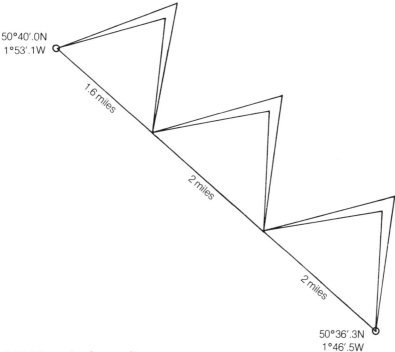

Fig 3.11 Measuring longer distances

To draw a straight line between two positions at opposite ends of a large chart, it is often convenient to fold over the edge of the chart so that it passes through both positions. The edge can now be used to draw the line.

Defining position

A position is defined either by its latitude and longitude or by its bearing and distance *from* a known landmark. A position of 50° 42'.8N 1° 49'.0W could also be defined as 104°T *from* Boscombe Pier 1.0M.

QUESTIONS

3.1   Plot a position 50° 35'.5N 1° 57'.5W. What is in this position?

3.2   Draw a line from a position 0.2M south of the beacon at the end of the groyne off Hengistbury Head to a position 0.2M south of the pierhead at Boscombe.

   a. How close does this line pass to the yellow buoy which is 1M from the groyne?

3.2b How close does the line pass to the yellow buoy off Boscombe Pier?

3.3a. What is the true direction of Bournemouth Pier from Handfast Point?
b. What is the distance from Handfast Point to Bournemouth Pier?
c. How long would it take a boat travelling at 4.5 knots to cover this distance?

3.4   Plot a position 218°T from Bournemouth pierhead 2.9M.

3.5   What is the latitude and longitude of a position 111°T from the flagstaff (FS) on Peveril Point 1.1M? (*Note:* The flagstaff is in position 50° 36'.4N 1° 56'.6W.)

Chapter Four

What Affects the Compass?

Variation

In *Chapter Three* we ignored the inner circle on the compass rose. The inner circle is the magnetic compass rose. A compass needle points towards magnetic north, not towards true or geographic north. The magnetic north pole is about 1000 nautical miles from the geographical North Pole: it is situated in the area of Hudson Bay, Canada. In practice to find direction we use a compass which contains a needle shaped magnet suspended so that it is free to rotate horizontally. This magnet rotates until it points towards magnetic north. Normally directions on the chart are relative to true north (as shown on the outer circle of the compass rose). The angular difference between true north and magnetic north is called **variation**, Fig 4.1.

The variation depends on geographical position and can be as much as 30° in certain areas of the world where small craft are likely to go. Because the magnetic north pole rotates slowly around the geographical North Pole, there is also a slight change every year in any one geographical position. When navigating we frequently measure direction using a magnetic compass. Before this magnetic direction is plotted on the chart it is converted to true. We are constantly correcting between magnetic bearings and courses and true bearings and courses; see *Chapter Ten*.

The variation, and the year to which it applies, is printed on a chart across the compass rose. Look at the compass rose in position 50° 41'.0N 1° 46'.5W: the variation is *5° 25'W (1987) decreasing about 9' annually*. However at the compass rose in position 50° 36'.3N 1° 46'.5W the variation is *5° 20'W*. As we tend to use variation corrected to the nearest degree, there is only likely to be a significant change of variation in voyages over 200 nautical miles.

In Poole Bay the variation was 5° 25'W in 1987 decreasing 9' annually. In 1989 it will have decreased by 18': so it will be 5° 07'W. In practice we would correct this to the nearest whole degree: 5°W.

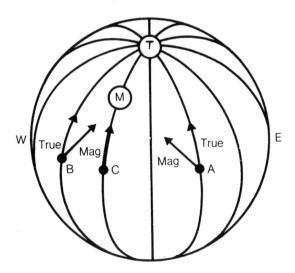

Fig 4.1 Variation – Magnetic north M is offset slightly from true north T, so the variation between the two will depend on where you are on the earth's surface in relation to them. At point B variation is East, at A it is West, whilst at C the variation is nil since true and magnetic north are directly in line.

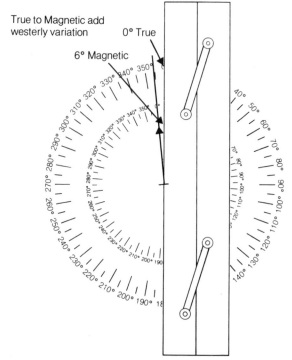

Fig 4.2 Applying variation

We need to remember whether to add or subtract variation when we are working between magnetic and true directions. Here is a way to remember. Refer to Fig 4.2. Place the parallel rule on the compass rose so that it passes through the figures 0°T and 180°T. The rule crosses the magnetic rose at 006°M (M for magnetic). So the magnetic direction is 6° greater than the true direction. The deflection is to the left or west. So we have a simple rule:

True to magnetic *add* variation west
Magnetic to true *subtract* variation west

Example 1a

True course	265°T	Magnetic course	148°M
Variation	+5°W	Variation	−7°W
Magnetic course	270°M	True course	141°T

To indicate a magnetic course or bearing the letter 'M' is placed after the figures. For variation east the rule is opposite to that for variation west:

True to magnetic *subtract* variation east
Magnetic to true *add* variation east

Example 1b

True course	111°T	Magnetic course	344°M
Variation	−3°E	Variation	+5°E
Magnetic course	108°M	True course	349°T

Deviation

A compass can also be affected by the close proximity of ferrous metal, electrical circuits and electronic equipment containing magnets. All of these produce influences that may cause the compass magnet to deflect from magnetic north. Any such deflection is called **deviation**.

The compass used by the helmsman is known as the **steering compass**. It is in a fixed position.

The site of the steering compass is important: the compass **heading** (the direction in which the boat is pointing) must be clearly visible to the helmsman; it must be firmly secured and in a safe position where it will not be damaged in heavy weather or by clumsy crew members; it should be well away from any deflecting influences; and the **lubber line** (the mark on the fixed part of the compass indicating the heading) must be accurately aligned with the fore-and-aft line of the boat.

For such a compass it is possible to compensate partly for any permanent magnetic influence by the location of magnetised needles adjacent to the compass; but this is a specialised task carried out by a qualified compass adjuster. The adjuster will manoeuvre the boat round in a circle measuring at regularly spaced headings the deviation of the steering compass: this procedure is known as a **compass swing**. Any remaining deviation will be tabulated for each compass heading in a **deviation table**. If the compass is re-sited, another compass swing is necessary. Deviation alters with a change of heading of the boat, so a deviation table will show the deviation to be applied for different headings of the boat, Fig 4.3. Deviation can be either east or west of magnetic north and corrections are applied using the same rules as for variation.

Compass Heading	Deviation
000°	5°E
020°	5°E
040°	4½°E
060°	4°E
080°	3½°E
100°	1½°W
120°	2½°W
140°	4°W
160°	5°W
180°	4½°W
200°	3½°W
220°	2°W
240°	0°
260°	2½°E
280°	4°E
300°	4½°E
320°	5°E
340°	5°E

Fig 4.3 Deviation table

A compass reading that has not been corrected for deviation or variation is shown by placing the letter 'C' after the figures.

Example 2a

Compass course	141°C	True course	057°T
Deviation	−4°W	Variation	+6°W
Magnetic course	137°M	Magnetic course	063°M
Variation	−5°W	Deviation	−4°E
True course	132°T	Compass course	059°C

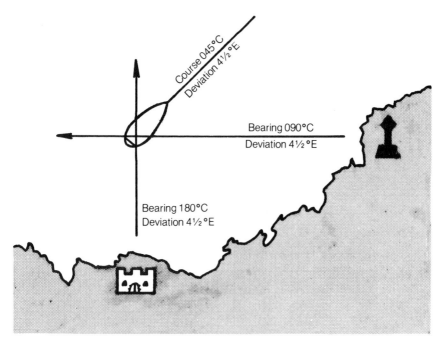

Fig 4.4 Deviation changes with the boat's heading, not with the bearings taken whilst on that heading. Thus if the deviation on heading 045°C is 4½E, the deviation remains 4½E for all bearings taken with the steering compass whilst on that heading

Compass error

If variation and deviation are aggregated together, the result is known as **compass error**.

Example 2b

Variation	6°W	True course	057°T
Deviation	−4°E	Compass error	+2°W
Compass error	2°W	Compass course	059°C

Hand-bearing compass

For taking bearings of landmarks, buoys and other vessels in the vicinity a separate hand-held compass is used. As it is not fitted in a permanent position, there can be no deviation table for it so it must be used in positions on a boat where there is negligible deviation. Any bearings taken with a hand-bearing compass are magnetic bearings.

If the course indicated on the steering compass is suspect, it can be checked against the direction of the boat's head using the hand-bearing compass. With the boat on a steady course, the hand-bearing compass is lined up with the fore-and-aft line of the boat and the readings of the two compasses compared.

Example 3

Steering compass	340°C
Hand-bearing compass	346°M
Deviation	6°E

QUESTIONS

4.1   What is the variation in Poole Bay in position 50° 40′N 1° 55′W for the year 1990?

4.2a.   Correct the following true bearings to magnetic bearings:

Bearing	Variation
218°T	6°W
147°T	4°E
359°T	10°W

b.   Correct the following magnetic bearings to true bearings:

Bearing	Variation
001°M	9°W
178°M	7°E
007°M	5°E

4.3a.   Correct the following magnetic bearings to compass bearings:

Bearing	Deviation
010°M	9°E
356°M	8°W
162°M	4°E

b.   Correct the following compass bearings to magnetic bearings:

Bearing	Deviation
241°C	10°W
054°C	12°E
292°C	3°W

4.4   A boat is on a course of 060°C. The variation is 6°W; the deviation is shown in Fig 4.3. The following bearings are taken using the steering compass:

Tower	091°C
Church	167°C
Monument	330°C

a. What are the true bearings to plot?
b. What is the compass error?

4.5 What should be taken into consideration when siting a compass?

Chapter Five

Reading the Shorthand

Chart symbols

In order to include navigational information on the chart but still leave it legible, many symbols and abbreviations are used. Some of these are self explanatory, Fig 5.1; but others need interpretation, Fig 5.2.

| Telephone | Yacht club |
| Fig 5.1 | Fig 5.2 |

Whilst a key may be included on some charts, generally it is necessary to refer to another publication such as *Symbols and Abbreviations used on Admiralty Charts*, which is Admiralty chart 5011 published in booklet form.

On chart 15 under the title there is an explanation of some of the symbols and abbreviations used. See if you can find the symbols shown in Fig 5.3.

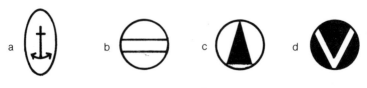

Fig 5.3

The symbols in Fig 5.3 are: Harbour office; Customs office; Marina; Visitor's berth.

Buoys are indicated by a small symbol showing their shape with letters to define their colour, Fig 5.4. Any light is shown by a magenta blob, Fig 5.5; the light characteristics being listed adjacent to the buoy symbol. The characteristics state: the number of times in a period that the light flashes or occults (goes out); the colour; and the length of the period, Fig 5.6.

Symbol	Description	Position on Stanfords Chart 15
G	Green conical shaped buoy	50°39'.9N 1°55'.4W

Fig 5.4

Symbol	Description	Position on Stanfords Chart 15
QG Bell G	Green conical shaped buoy with a conical shaped topmark, a green quick flashing light and a bell	50°39'.4N 1°55'.2W

Fig 5.5

Symbol	Description	Position on Stanfords Chart 15
Fl(2) R 10s	Red can shaped buoy with a can shaped top mark and a red light showing two flashes every 10 seconds	50°39'.3N 1°58'.0W

Fig 5.6

The positions of lighthouses and lights on land used for navigation are shown by a star augmented by the magenta blob, Fig 5.7. For these, additional information on sectored lights, height of light, luminous range of the light and fog signalling apparatus are included.

Symbol	Description	Position on Stanfords Chart 15
Fl 10s 45m 24M Horn(3) 30s	Lighthouse with a white light flashing every 10 seconds. It is 45 metres high. The light is visible for 24 miles. In bad visibility a horn sounds three blasts every 30 seconds	50°35'.5N 1°57'.5W

Fig 5.7

Some heights of easily identifiable or conspicuous (*conspic*) land-marks (churches, towers, chimneys, radio masts) are given, Fig 5.8. Such heights are shown in brackets, e.g. (21), and are in metres above a datum level called **mean high water springs** (MHWS) which is defined in Chapter Six.

In anchorages the quality of the sea-bed is indicated, Fig 5.9.

Depths of water (below the datum level of the chart) are shown in metres and tenths of metre, Fig 5.10. A **drying height**, which is the height to which a rock or sandbank would be exposed if the sea level fell to the datum level of the chart, has the same basic abbreviation as a charted depth but, in addition, the number indicating metres is underlined, Fig 5.11.

Tidal stream data is keyed to a specific position using a tidal dia-mond, Fig 5.12.

Symbol	Description	Position on Stanfords Chart 15
	Old Harry rock is 18 metres above MHWS	50°36'.5N 1°55'.2W

Fig 5.8

Sm St bk Sh	Small stones, broken shells	50°38'.7N 1°55'.4W

Fig 5.9

16_4	Depth below chart datum	50°41'.7N 1°44'.2W

Fig 5.10

$\underline{0}_7$	Drying height	50°38'.9N 1°56.9W

Fig 5.11

⟨C⟩	Tidal diamond	50°39'.2N 1°54'.9W

Fig 5.12

Chart corrections

As well as keeping a chart up-to-date, it is important to be able to know that a chart has been fully corrected. Commercial publishers from time to time issue a list of corrections, or a chart can be returned for updating. However the trend is to re-issue a chart at regular intervals.

Corrections to Admiralty charts are promulgated in a weekly bulletin known as the *Admiralty Notices to Mariners (weekly edition).* Each Notice lists all the charts (and publications) affected together with the number of the Notice with the last correction. When a correction is made, the year and number of the Notice are noted in the bottom left-hand corner of the chart. If the last correction was not shown, then it could be incorporated. For United Kingdom waters a 'small craft' edition of the *Admiralty Notices to Mariners* is published (four times a year) which only includes corrections to home waters charts.

QUESTIONS

5.1 What publication shows chart symbols and abbreviations?

5.2a. Using chart 15, identify the following:

1   2   3

b. What chart symbols are in the following positions:

| 50° 40'.6N | 50° 38'.7N | 50° 40'.9N |
| 1° 56'.3W | 1° 55'.8W | 1° 56'.7W |

c. What is the quality of the bottom in position 50° 38'.7N 1° 55'.8W?

5.3 Draw a line from 50° 38'.7N 1° 56'.0W to 135°T Training Bank beacon 0.1M. What is the minimum charted depth along this line?

5.4 What is the significance of the wavy lines in position 50° 35'.3N 1° 56'.5W?

5.5 What is the height of Anvil Point light?

Chapter Six

What Causes the Tides?

Tides are vertical movements of water caused by combinations of the gravitational pull of the sun and the moon.

Each day around the British Isles there are normally two high tides when the sea-level reaches its highest point, called high water (HW), and two low tides when the sea-level is at its lowest point, called low water (LW). A rising tide (flood tide) is the period between LW and HW, and a falling tide (ebb tide) the period from HW to LW. The height difference between HW and the preceding or succeeding LW is called the **range**; and the time difference is called the **duration**. The difference from HW or LW to any given time is known as the **interval**. The depth of water shown on a chart (the **charted depth** or **sounding**) is the depth of the seabed below the chart datum which is the lowest level to which the tide is expected to fall due to astronomical conditions (**Lowest Astronomical Tide** or **LAT**).

The tide level does not rise and fall by the same amount each day. Over a period of approximately two weeks the heights of high water and low water vary from a minimum to a maximum then back to a minimum. The combination of the highest high water and the lowest low water (maximum range) is called a **spring** tide; and the combination of the lowest high water and the highest low water (minimum range) a **neap** tide, Fig 6.1. During one four week period there will be two spring tides and two neap tides.

At the time of the equinoxes (21st March and 21st September) when the earth and the sun are closest together, the spring tides have the greatest range and are known as **equinoctial spring tides**.

The height of a tide can be affected by weather conditions. If the barometric pressure is high (1040mb) over a period of several days, the increased pressure of the air on the sea surface can lower the sea-level by as much as 0.3 metres. A strong wind blowing into an estuary over a period of several days can raise the sea-level by a similar

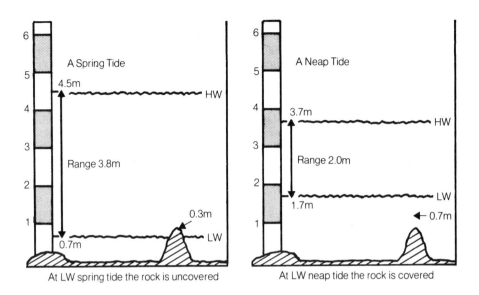

Fig 6.1 Spring and neap tides

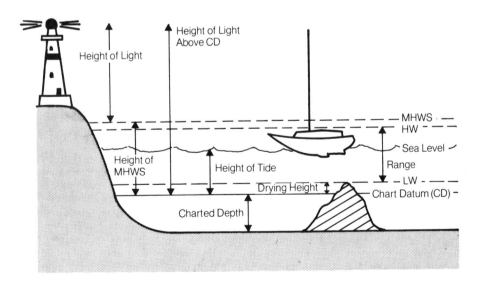

Fig 6.2 Datum levels

amount; or conversely lower it if the wind is blowing out to sea. Under these circumstances variations in predicted heights and times of high and low water can occur.

Datum levels

We have defined **chart datum** or **CD** as the lowest level to which the tide is expected to fall due to astronomical conditions. Other datum levels are shown in Fig 6.2. They are all 'mean' (average) levels taken over a period of one year: mean high water springs (MHWS) being the mean height above chart datum of the high waters of spring tides. Certain yachtsman's almanacs use mean high water (MHW) or mean low water (MLW) being the mean level of all the high waters or low waters over a period of one year. Mean high water springs (MHWS) is used as the datum level for heights of land features. For comparison with the heights of land features shown on maps, large scale charts and tide tables include the differences between chart datum and the ordnance survey datum for various locations.

QUESTIONS

6.1   What is chart datum?

6.2   Can the tide ever fall below chart datum?

6.3a.   What is charted depth?
    b.   How is this shown on chart 15?

6.4   What datum level is used when indicating the height of land features?

6.5   When does the greatest range of tide occur?

Chapter Seven

How Much Water is There?

Information on tides is found in *Admiralty Tide Tables*, a yachtsman's almanac or local tide tables. There are tables which show the times and heights of high water and low water at main ports (called **standard ports**). For other ports, known as **secondary ports**, the times and heights of high water and low water are found by corrections to the adjacent standard port times and heights. These corrections, known as **secondary port differences**, are found in a separate set of tables. Some local tide tables incorporate these differences.

The tables only give the height of the tide at the time of high water and low water. To find out the height of tide at other times, diagrams of **tidal curves** are used. There are tidal curves for each standard port; and, with certain exceptions, the same tidal curves are used for the associated secondary ports.

To understand how to use the tide tables and tidal curves we will work through some examples. All heights are in metres and all times are indicated using a four figure notation based on a 24 hour day. Times shown are in local mean time (UK: GMT). During summer months 1 hour must be added (UK: BST).

Standard ports

To find the time for a given height of tide at a standard port.
Use Extract 1 p. 118 for Examples 4 and 5.

Example 4
At what time (BST) at Dover during the afternoon of 2nd June will the tide rise to a height of 3.2m?
For the period covering the afternoon of 2nd June, extract from the tide tables for the port of Dover the times and heights of high water (HW) and low water (LW) and work out the range by subtracting the height of LW from the height of HW. Convert all times to BST.

	LW		HW		
	Time	Height	Time	Height	Range
Dover	0915 GMT	1.6	1427 GMT	5.8	4.2
Add 1 hour	+0100		+0100		
Dover	1015 BST		1527 BST		

Refer to the tidal curve diagram, Fig 7.1.

1. Fill in on the time scale at the bottom of the tidal curve diagram the time of HW (1527) and hours before and after HW as required.
2. Mark the height of HW (5.8) on the top height scale (H.W.Hts.m) and the height of LW (1.6) on the bottom height scale (L.W.Hts.m).
3. Draw the range line between the HW mark and the LW mark.
4. Mark the height of tide required (3.2) on the top height scale and draw a line vertically downwards to the range line.
5. From the point of intersection on the range line draw a horizontal line to the right to cut the rising or falling curve as appropriate. It may be necessary to interpolate between the curves for spring and neap ranges. Compare the range (4.2) with the mean ranges shown in the top right-hand corner of the tidal curve diagram: springs 5.9m, neaps 3.3m. In this case the range (4.2) is halfway (0.5) between the mean ranges for springs and neaps. (Do not extrapolate outside the curves on the diagram.)
6. Draw a line vertically downwards from the tidal curve to the time scale and read off the interval: HW−2h 50m. Apply this interval to the time of HW to give the time required of 1237.

(*Note:* An interval is shown as before or after HW by the use of a − or + sign.)

To find the height of tide at a given time at a standard port.

Example 5
What will be the height of tide at Dover on 17th May at 1100 BST?
For the period including 1100 on 17th May, extract the times and heights of high water and low water from the tide tables for Dover and work out the range.

	LW		HW		
	Time	Height	Time	Height	Range
Dover	0833 GMT	0.9	1341 GMT	6.2	5.3
Add 1 hour	+0100		+0100		(0.2 from
Dover	0933 BST		1441 BST		springs)

Refer to the tidal curve diagram, Fig 7.2.

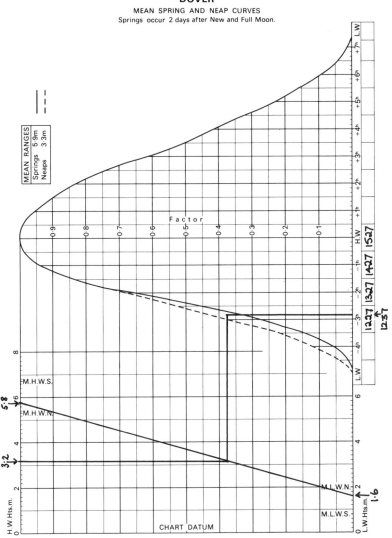

DOVER
MEAN SPRING AND NEAP CURVES
Springs occur 2 days after New and Full Moon.

Fig 7.1

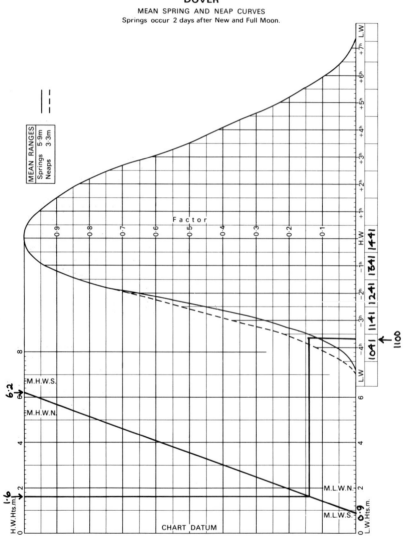

DOVER

MEAN SPRING AND NEAP CURVES

Springs occur 2 days after New and Full Moon.

Fig 7.2

Proceed as for Example 4 as far as step 3.

4. Enter the time scale with the interval HW−3h 41m (1100) and draw a line vertically upwards to the tidal curve interpolating if necessary between the spring and neap curves.

5. From this point on the tidal curve, draw a horizontal line to the left to the range line.

6. From the point of intersection on the range line draw a line vertically upwards to the height scale and read off the height which is 1.6m.

(*Note:* Although we have extracted the time of LW, it is not required in any calculation so it can be ignored.)

Secondary ports

To find the time that the tide will reach a given height at a secondary port.
Use Extracts 1 and 2 p. 118 for Examples 6 and 7

Example 6
At what time (BST) will the tide first fall to a height of 2.5m at Ramsgate on 16th May?
For the period covering the falling tide on 16th May, extract the times and heights of high water and low water at the standard port, Dover. From the tide tables work out the range, then apply the tidal differences for the secondary port, Ramsgate.

	HW		LW		
	Time	Height	Time	Height	Range
Dover	0017 GMT	6.4	0745 GMT	0.8	5.6
Differences	+0020	−1.6	−0007	−0.6	(nearly
Ramsgate	0037 GMT	4.8	0738 GMT	0.2	springs)
Add 1 hour	+0100		+0100		
Ramsgate	0137 BST		0838 BST		

Refer to the tidal curve diagram, Fig 7.3.

The tidal curve diagram for the standard port is used as in Examples 4 and 5 but the times and heights of HW and LW at the secondary port are entered on the diagram. The range at the *standard* port is required for the interpolation between the spring and neap curves. The interval is HW+3h 30m. The time required is 0507.

(*Note:* The time correction to BST is made *after* the differences for the secondary port have been applied.)

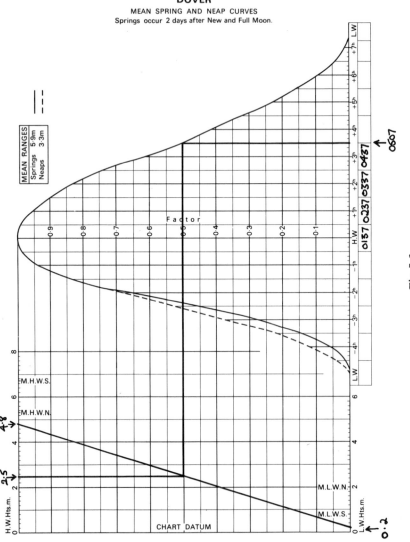

DOVER
MEAN SPRING AND NEAP CURVES
Springs occur 2 days after New and Full Moon.

Fig 7.3

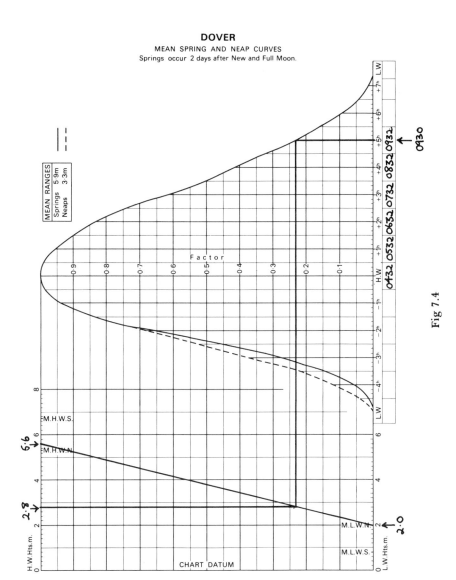

DOVER
MEAN SPRING AND NEAP CURVES
Springs occur 2 days after New and Full Moon.

Fig 7.4

To find the height of tide at a given time at a secondary port.

Example 7
What will be the height of tide at Folkestone on 4th June at 0930 BST?

	HW		LW		
	Time	Height	Time	Height	Range
Dover	0342 GMT	5.2	1041 GMT	2.0	3.2
Differences	−0010	+0.4	−0010	0.0	(neaps)
Folkestone	0032 GMT	5.6	1031 GMT	2.0	
Add 1 hour	+0100		+0100		
Folkestone	0432 BST		1131 BST		

Refer to tidal curve diagram, Fig 7.4.

Height required: 2.8m

Solent ports (Swanage to Selsey)

Look at Fig 7.5 which is the tidal curve diagram for Lymington and
Yarmouth both of which come under the special classification of
Solent ports. What are the differences between this diagram and the
tidal curve diagram for Dover, Fig 7.1? There are two differences:
Lymington and Yarmouth are both secondary ports, the standard
port for the area being Portsmouth; and the time intervals are from
LW rather than HW.

In the area covered by the Solent ports the tides are complex with
the result that HW can remain at a steady level (called a stand of the
tide) or occasionally fall a little then rise again for a second HW. The
tidal pattern varies considerably between ports adjacent to each
other. Therefore it is much easier to determine the time of LW
rather than HW and so tidal curve diagrams use LW as the datum. As
the tidal patterns of the secondary ports are so different to the standard port, Portsmouth, and to each other, a complete series of tidal
curve diagrams is necessary. Poole Harbour, though not formally a
standard port, has its own set of tide tables.

A slightly modified procedure is used with the tidal curve diagrams for Solent ports.

To find the time for a given height of tide at a Solent port.
Use Extracts 3 and 4 pp. 119–20 for Examples 8 and 9

Example 8
*At what time in the afternoon of 1st May will the tide at Lymington fall to a
height of 1.8m?*
For the afternoon of 1st May, extract the time and height of low

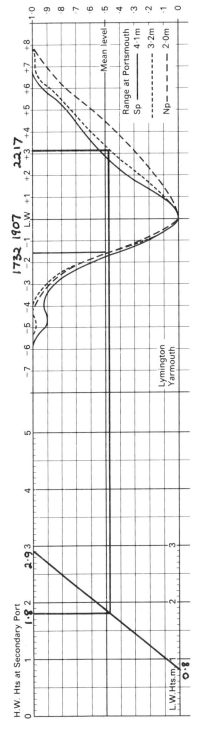

Fig 7.5

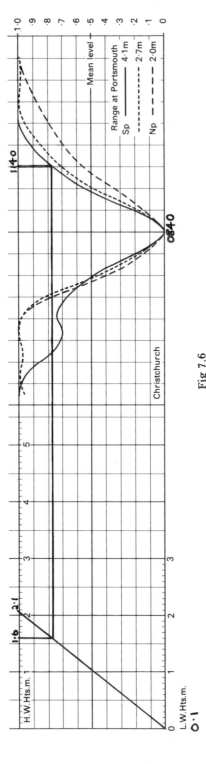

Fig 7.6

water and the height of high water for the standard port, Portsmouth, and apply the tidal differences from Lymington.

	HW Height	LW Time	Height	Range
Portsmouth	4.4	1827 GMT	1.1	3.3
Differences	−1.5	−0020	−0.3	(mid range)
Lymington	2.9	1807 GMT	0.8	
Add 1 hour		+0100		
Lymington		1907 BST		

Refer to tidal curve diagram, Fig 7.5.

Fill in the time of LW and the heights of HW and LW. Compare the range of tide at Portsmouth with the spring, neap and mid ranges shown on the tidal curve diagram to determine which curve to use. Proceed as for previous examples for secondary ports.

Interval: LW−1h 35m.
Time required: 1732.

To find the height of tide at a given time for a Solent port.

Example 9
What is the height of tide at Christchurch on 16th July at 1140 BST?

	LW Time	Height	HW Height	Range
Portsmouth	0815 GMT	0.8	4.7	3.9
Differences	−0035	−0.7	−2.6	(springs)
Christchurch	0740 GMT	0.1	2.1	
Add 1 hour	+0100			
Christchurch	0840 BST			
Interval: LW+3h 00m				

Refer to tidal curve diagram, Fig 7.6.
Height of tide required: 1.6m

Clearances

With the knowledge of the height of tide at a particular location, examination of the depths of water and drying heights shown on the chart will enable the actual depth of water to be determined. If the draught of the boat is known, then the clearance between the bottom of the keel and the seabed can be worked out, Fig 7.7.

If the information on the chart is dubious or lacking, the depth

determined from the echo-sounder or lead line can be used to estimate the charted depth. To allow for any rounding in the tidal calcu-
lations and for any abnormal weather conditions, a minimum clearance of 0.5m between the keel and the seabed is normally assumed.

Example 10
A motor yacht whose draught is 1.1m anchors in the approaches to Lymington
River at 1732 BST on 1st May. At that time the depth of water was 1.7m as
measured on the echo-sounder which was sited 0.3m below the waterline. Will
she be aground at low water; and how much anchor chain should she let out if
she intends to remain overnight?

Refer to Fig 7.7 and Example 8.

Example 8 shows that the height of tide at Lymington at 1732 on 1st
May is 1.8m on a falling tide. LW is at 1907 and the height of tide at
LW is 0.8m. If the echo-sounder is 0.3m below the waterline and
indicates 1.7m, then the actual depth of water at 1732 is 2.0m. The
seabed is therefore $2.0-1.8=0.2$m below chart datum (this means
the charted depth would be shown as 0_2). The height of tide at LW is
0.8m above chart datum or $0.8+0.2=1.0$m above the seabed. As the
motor yacht draws 1.1m, *she will be aground at LW*. At the following
HW the height of tide will be 2.9m above chart datum or
$2.9+0.2=3.1$M above the seabed. The rule of thumb to determine

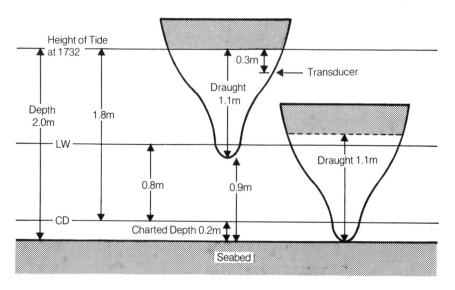

Fig 7.7 At 1732 the boat has a clearance above the sea bed of 0.9m but at LW
she will be aground

the length of anchor chain to let out is 3× maximum depth of water in calm weather or 3×3.1 =9.3m; so 10m of anchor chain would be on the safe side.

Example 11
In Lymington River a boat goes aground on a falling tide at 1732 BST on 1st May. At what time might she expect to refloat?
Refer to Example 8 and tidal curve diagram, Fig 7.5.

In simple terms the question asks 'When will the height of tide return to the same level that it was at 1732'. On Fig 7.5 if the horizontal line is extended to the right to cut the mid range curve on the rising tide, and a line drawn vertically upwards, then this line will cut the time scale at LW+3h 10m or 2217.

Example 12
In the morning of 16th July a motor yacht with a draught of 1.2m wishes to leave Christchurch harbour with a clearance of at least 0.5m over the bar at the entrance. What is the earliest time she can leave?
Refer to Example 9 and chart 15.

The inset on chart 15 for Christchurch harbour shows a depth over the bar at the entrance of 0.1m (0_1). The least depth of water required by the motor yacht is 1.2+0.5=1.7m. The height of tide required will be 1.7−0.1=1.6m. Example 9 shows that this height of tide will be reached at 1140 BST.

Heights of land features

All heights of land features are measured above the datum level of Mean High Water Springs (MHWS), Fig 6.2. Heights of features are in metres and are shown on the chart enclosed in brackets (18) (see Fig 5.8). The characteristics of lighthouses and lightships include the height of the light in metres above MHWS shown as a number followed by the letter 'm'. For Anvil Point light the characteristics are: Fl 10s 45m 24M Horn(3) 30s. The height of the light is 45 metres above MHWS. The nominal range of the light is 24 nautical miles (24M). The **nominal range** of a light is the range at which it will be sighted when the normal meteorological visibility is 10M. It is really a measure of the brightness of the light.

Distance off when raising a light

The characteristics of a lighthouse show the height of the light above MHWS; which, for Anvil Point light, is 45m. The height of MHWS above chart datum can be determined from the tide datum levels shown on a chart. If the height of tide is also calculated, then the height of a light above sea level can be worked out. Tables can be found in yachtsman's almanacs showing the 'distance off' of a light when it is first seen (or raised) on the horizon. To use these tables the observer must know his 'height of eye' above sea level; which, for a small craft, is usually 1.5m to 2.0m. For instance, at the time of high water, Anvil Point light would be raised from a boat with the height of the eye of the observer at 1.5m above sea level at a distance off of 16.5M.

See Extract 5 p. 120: Distance off a light

At night, particularly if the conditions are cloudy, the loom (reflected beam) of the light from a lighthouse can be seen considerably beyond the point at which the light itself becomes visible. Similarly the street lights of a port well over the horizon may appear as a dim glow in the sky.

QUESTIONS

For questions 7.3, 7.4, 7.5 use Extracts 1, 2, 3, 4 pp. 118–20 and Figs 7.1, 7.5

7.1   Where can information be obtained on times and heights of tides?

7.2   A boat with a draught of 2.0m needs a clearance of 0.5m to cross a sandbar which dries 1.3m. What is the height of tide required?

7.3   What is the height of tide at Dover on 17th June at 1920 BST?

7.4   At what time (BST) during the afternoon of 1st June will the tide first reach a height of 2.5m at Ramsgate?

7.5   What is the height of tide at Yarmouth at 1015 BST on 2nd June?

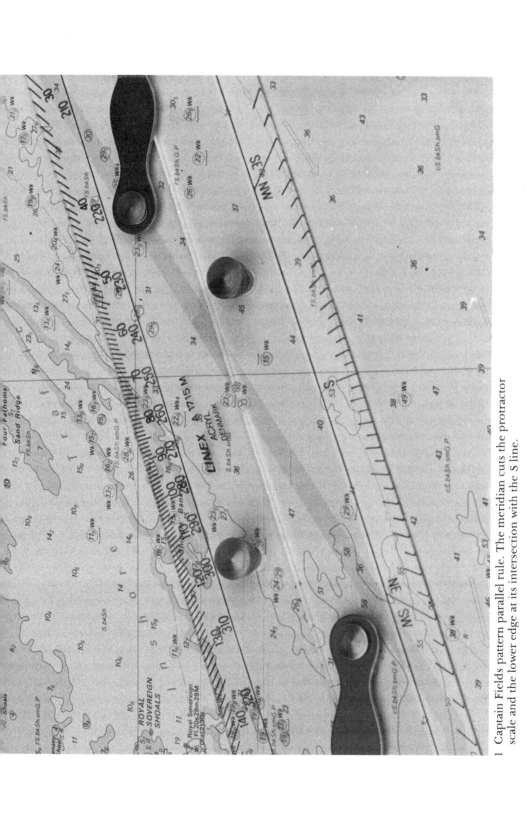

1 Captain Fields pattern parallel rule. The meridian cuts the protractor scale and the lower edge at its intersection with the S line.

Above: 2 Poole Fairway buoy marks the entrance to Poole. The training bank (outer end) beacon is visible on the port hand and the Haven Hotel in the distance. Buoy: safe water.

Below: 3 Leading line. Entrance to Beaulieu river showing leading line over the bar. The rear mark is occasionally obscured by the trees.

Right: 4 Christchurch Harbour entrance. The buoy is laid from May to October to indicate deep water over the bar. Buoy: port hand (secondary).

Above: 5 Groyne off Hengistbury Head. Red can shaped beacon at southern end. Port hand beacon.

Below: 6 CG lookout – Hengistbury Head.

Above: 7 Christchurch Priory. View from a point to the west of Hengistbury Head. Buoy: yellow non-navigational.

Below: 8 Water tower (conspic). Becomes obscured by the cliff if the observer is closer to the shore.

Above: 9 Bournemouth – St Peter's church. St Peter's church is just open to the left of Bournemouth pier.
Left: 10 Bournemouth – hotel (conspic). Chine with beach below the hotel. Buoy: yellow non-navigational.
Below: 11 Poole Fairway – Handfast Point. Poole Fairway buoy is almost in transit with Handfast Point. Old Harry Rock is not clearly visible. Buoy: safe water.

Above: 12 Handfast Point – Durlston Head. Durlston Head is just open off Old Harry Rock.

Below: 13 Handfast Point. Old Harry Rock does not stand out. The anchorage in Studland Bay is visible beyond Old Harry's wife.

Above: 14 Peveril Ledge – Durlston Head. The castle is visible on Durlston Head. There are frequently extensive overfalls on the ebb tide around the buoy: port hand buoy.

Below: 15 Peveril Point. Ledge, Coastguard lookout and flagstaff on Peveril Point with castle on Durlston Head in background.

Above: 16 Swanage pier. Methodist church (with spire) and anchorage.
Below: 17 Swanage town. Transit of methodist church and monument.
Right: 18 Anvil Point. Further to the north the lighthouse becomes obscured.

Above: 19 Ballard Point. Handfast Point in distance.

Below: 20 Haven Hotel. Marine radiobeacon is the mast on the roof at the right-hand side of the hotel.

Above: 21 East Looe channel. Inward bound from East Looe buoy, leave the N cardinal beacon to port and N Haven Point about 100 yards to starboard: port hand buoy.

Below: 22 Chain ferry. Note black ball (lowered) on the ferry. The ferry should be given a wide berth.

23 Bell buoy. Brownsea Road. The buoy marks the division between the Mid Ship channel to port and the North channel: south cardinal buoy.

Above: 24 Ro-Ro Terminal. Power station chimneys in background.

Below: 25 No 67 Buoy. Off Poole Yacht Club. Leading line beacons can be seen on left hand side of picture amongst small boat moorings: starboard hand buoy.

Above: 26 No 76 Buoy. A line of port hand buoys across Wareham Lake leads to the River Frome. Buoy: port hand (secondary).

Below: 27 Poole Bridge. The lifting bridge in Poole town leading to Cobbs Quay and Holes Bay.

Chapter Eight

Tidal Stream: Fair or Foul?

The vertical rise and fall of the tide is the result of the horizontal movement of water known as a **tidal stream**. For specific positions on each chart there is a table which gives the true direction *towards* which the tidal stream is flowing together with the rate of flow in knots (nautical miles per hour) for both spring and neap tides. This information is tabulated for the time of high water at the associated standard port and at hourly intervals before and after. The specific positions are indicated by a diamond shape enclosing a letter: they are known as **tidal diamonds**, Fig 5.12.

Tidal stream diamonds

Refer to the tidal stream tabulation for tidal diamond B on chart 15. At HW (high water) the tidal stream at tidal diamond B will be setting in the direction 179°T at a rate of 0.8 knots for a spring tide and 0.4 knots for a neap tide. A boat travelling on a southerly course (180°T) would be assisted by this tidal stream which is said to be **fair**. For a boat travelling towards the north the passage time would be increased and this tidal stream is said to be **foul**. For a boat travelling east or west the tidal stream will be across the track and must be allowed for in determination of the course to steer. Later we will use the information from these tidal diamonds when we determine, by plotting on the chart, the effect of the tidal stream on the track of the boat.

For example, use tidal diamond B, HW Portsmouth 1300, springs. The direction and rate tabulated are mean values for one hour, so for the period from 0730 to 0830 the mean tidal stream would be 346°T 1.2k (HW−5). For the period from 0830 to 0930 the tidal stream would be 354°T 1.0k (HW−4). If, however, the tidal stream is required for the period from 0800 to 0900, then it would be necessary to use 30 minutes from the tidal stream tabulated for

49

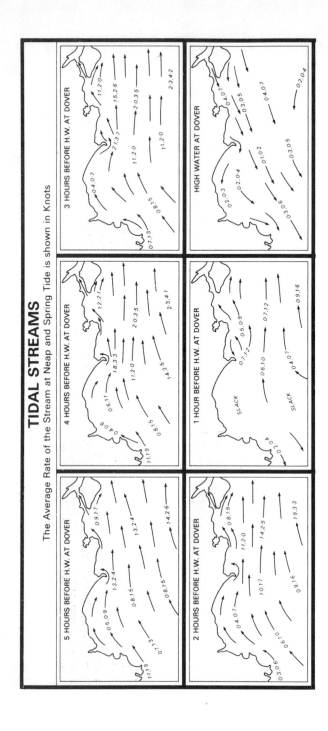

TIDAL STREAMS

The Average Rate of the Stream at Neap and Spring Tide is shown in Knots

Fig 8.1

HW−5 (346°T 0.6M) and 30 minutes from that tabulated for HW−4 (354°T 0.5M).

Tidal stream atlas

Tidal streams are also represented pictorially in a **tidal stream atlas** or **tidal stream diagram**, Fig 8.1.

Tidal stream atlases or diagrams are used either for passage planning or for pilotage. The arrow indicates the direction of flow. The figures are divided by the dot in the centre: the larger number representing the spring rate and the smaller the neap rate. (On Admiralty Tidal Stream Atlases the rates are multiplied by 10 for convenience: 12.24 is a neap rate of 1.2 knots and a spring rate of 2.4 knots.)

All the figures shown for rates of flow are mean rates; they can vary considerably at exceptional spring tides.

Effects of tidal streams

There is normally no tidal stream information for areas close inshore. Sometimes information on local effects is given in naviga-

Fig 8.2 A good look at anchored vessels, buoys etc. will enable you to estimate the speed and direction of the tidal stream

tion guidebooks known as 'sailing directions' or 'pilots'.

Generally a tidal stream does not flow as strongly in shallow water; and in a bay it may sweep round in a contrary direction to the main stream. However it tends to flow faster around headlands, sometimes causing severe tide races or overfalls where the water is very confused: see symbols on chart 15 in the vicinity of Durlston Head (50° 35'.6N 1° 57'.0W). It can also well up from an uneven bottom causing disturbed seas and eddies. These areas should be avoided particularly if the wind is blowing in the opposite direction to the tidal stream.

Every opportunity should be taken to observe the direction and rate of the tidal stream when passing moored boats, buoys and lobster pots, Fig 8.2.

In a river or tidal estuary the strongest current or tidal stream, and the deepest water, lie on the outside of a bend; the inside frequently silts up. In the absence of any buoys, beacons or withies, do not cut the corners on bends.

A tidal stream flowing over a shallow bank often produces a standing wave just downstream of the bank. Keep well clear of any such standing waves.

QUESTIONS

Use chart 15

8.1   What is the direction and rate of the tidal stream at spring tides one hour after high water in position 50° 39'N 1° 55'W?

8.2   In relation to high water when is the tidal stream east-going in the English Channel off Portland Bill (use Fig 8.1)?

8.3   At spring tides in the area covered by tidal diamond A the tidal stream was flowing faster than tabulated. Why might this be?

8.4   The tidal stream at tidal diamond B is 026° 0.3k. The wind is from the west. The boats at anchor in Studland Bay are lying with their bows pointing west. Why?

8.5   Approaching Poole Fairway buoy, how can you check on the direction of the tidal stream?

Chapter Nine

Pilotage: Finding the Way Without Plotting

When making a short passage relatively close to the shore in good visibility, the navigator relies on what he can see to establish his position and to work out the direction to go. There is often little opportunity for regular chartwork. There are many landmarks: such as headlands, lighthouses, churches, water towers. There are also buoys and beacons. Using these as signposts to establish the boat's present position and where to go next is **pilotage**. Should the visibility deteriorate and the signposts disappear, then it will be necessary to start plotting on the chart; and pilotage becomes navigation.

Referring to chart 15, let us imagine that we are in a yacht entering Poole Harbour from a position of 50° 39'.2N 1° 54'.8W close to the Poole Fairway buoy. It is a sunny day, the visibility is good, there is a light following breeze and there is a flood tide (so both the wind and tide are fair). The boat's speed is 4 knots. Looking to the north-west we can see the harbour entrance by the Haven Hotel in the distance and the Training Bank (outer end) beacon off to port. The chart shows the twin lines of green (starboard hand) and red (port hand) buoys leading towards the entrance (Plate 2). Keeping to the right of the channel (in accordance with the rules of the road) it is easy to sail from one green buoy to the next. Measure the distance from the Fairway buoy to the harbour entrance: it is about 2.3M (nautical miles). At 4 knots with a fair tidal stream we should reach the entrance in 30 minutes. We can then enter the harbour; but watch out for the chain ferry!

Lights and lighthouses

Lights used for navigational purposes are indicated with a magenta blob. They may be in magnificent lighthouses or they may be sited in the windows of buildings. Often the light can be easily seen at night, but the light structure cannot be identified by day. Two lights

Fig 9.1 The Conventional Direction of Buoyage in the British Isles follows the arrows shown

in transit (leading lights) offer an ideal method of keeping within a channel (particularly if some of the buoys are unlit). Sometimes a single light will have an intensified sector on a certain bearing that marks the centre of a channel. Lights may be sectored (White, Red, Green) to indicate potential hazards. The light in position 50° 41'.1N 1° 56'.4W marks the East Looe channel into Poole harbour. Its characteristic on chart 15 is shown as Oc WRG 6s 9m 10,6M. In *Extract 6*, see page 121, the sectors are given: Red 234°–294°; White 294°–304°; Green 304°–024°. By convention the bearings shown are true directions as observed from *seaward*. The nominal range of the white light is 10M, and of the red and green lights 6M.

Buoys and beacons

Buoys are plentiful in the approaches to commercial ports. For smaller harbours and secondary channels beacons are used extensively. Occasionally, down infrequently used channels, tree branches (called withies) are stuck in the mud to indicate the deep water. When a vessel is proceeding in the general direction of the buoyage or into harbour, buoys marking the channel will be green conical shaped to starboard and red can-shaped to port Fig 9.1. Beacons will be green with conical shaped topmarks to starboard and red with can shaped topmarks to port. Figs 9.2 to 9.9 and Plates 2, 4, 5, 7, 10, 14, 21, 23, 25, 26 show buoys and beacons used to mark channels and dangers.

For an unfamiliar passage, where a buoyed channel is to be followed, it is a good idea to draw up a list of the buoys (or beacons) in the order that they will be seen. Sufficient characteristics should

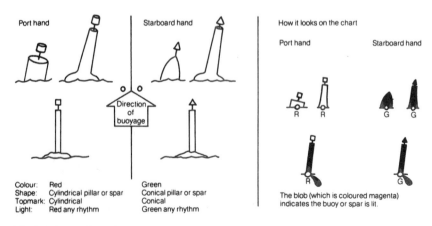

Fig 9.2 Lateral marks

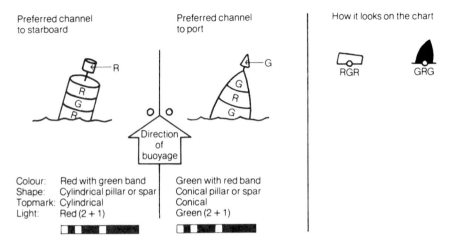

At the point where a channel divides lateral marks
may be modified by a horizontal green or red band.

Fig 9.3 Preferred channel marks

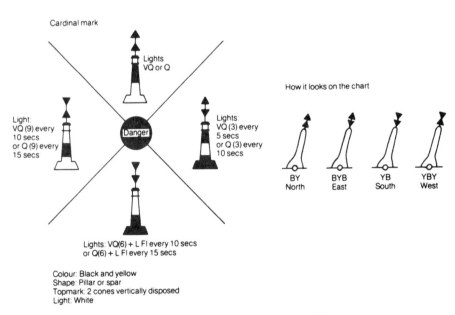

These marks are positioned to the north, east, south or west of danger.

Fig 9.4 Cardinal marks

How it looks on the chart

BRB

Colour: Red and black horizontal bands
Shape: Pillar or spar
Topmark: 2 spheres vertically disposed
Light: White, group flashing (2)

This mark is over an isolated danger where there is navigable water all around it.

Fig 9.5 Isolated danger

How it looks on the chart

RW   RW   RW

Colour: Red and white vertical stripes
Shape: Spherical pillar or spar
Topmark: Red sphere
Light: White-isophase,   occulting   or   morse letter A

This mark indicates that there is safe water around it.

Fig 9.6 Safe water mark

How it looks on the chart

Y   Y   Y

Colour: Yellow
Shape: Optional
Topmark: Cross
Light: Yellow

These are not navigational marks but have a special meaning which may be indicated on the chart. The shape is optional but must not conflict with navigational marks in the area.

Fig 9.7 Special mark

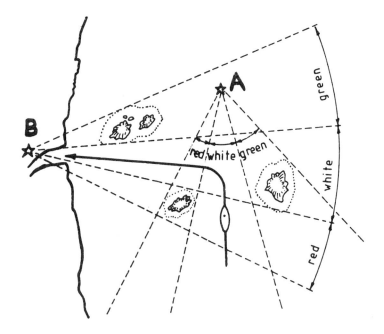

Fig 9.8 Sectored lights. Many lights have sectors of different colour: here the vessel must keep in the white sector of light A until she reaches the white sector of light B, when she can turn to port

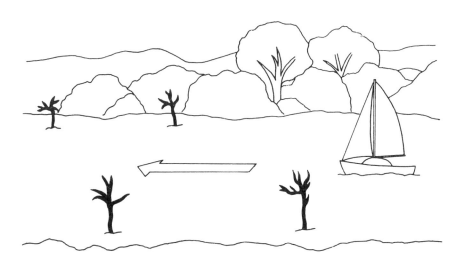

Fig 9.9 Withies. Further up the river: tree branches may be stuck in the mud to mark the edge of the channel

be included so that it will not be necessary to keep returning to the chart table. If there is any doubt about visibility, the direction and distance of the next mark (buoy or beacon) should be noted, Fig 9.10.

At night particular attention needs to be paid to the light characteristics of those buoys and beacons that are lit, Fig 9.11. From low down in a boat it is very difficult to judge distances, so the lights

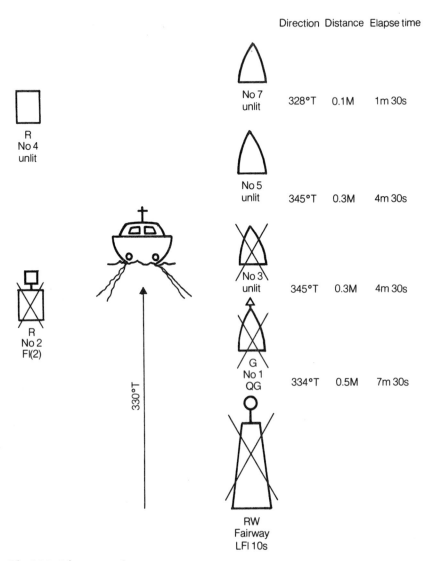

	Direction	Distance	Elapse time
No 7 unlit	328°T	0.1M	1m 30s
No 5 unlit	345°T	0.3M	4m 30s
No 3 unlit	345°T	0.3M	4m 30s
No 1 G QG	334°T	0.5M	7m 30s

R
No 4
unlit

R
No 2
Fl(2)

330°T

RW
Fairway
LFl 10s

Fig 9.10 A buoyage plan

must be ticked off (on our list) as they are passed. A watch with a second hand (or a digital stop watch) is useful for checking the characteristics of lights. Remember, too, that lights on buoys are not often visible at distances greater than two nautical miles. If the colour of a light is not indicated it is assumed to be white.

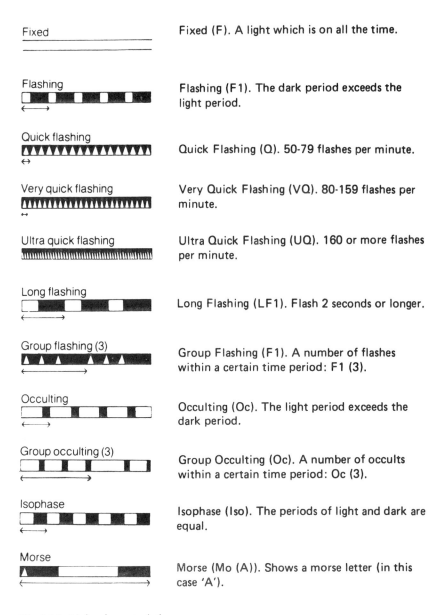

Fixed — Fixed (F). A light which is on all the time.

Flashing — Flashing (F1). The dark period exceeds the light period.

Quick flashing — Quick Flashing (Q). 50-79 flashes per minute.

Very quick flashing — Very Quick Flashing (VQ). 80-159 flashes per minute.

Ultra quick flashing — Ultra Quick Flashing (UQ). 160 or more flashes per minute.

Long flashing — Long Flashing (LF1). Flash 2 seconds or longer.

Group flashing (3) — Group Flashing (F1). A number of flashes within a certain time period: F1 (3).

Occulting — Occulting (Oc). The light period exceeds the dark period.

Group occulting (3) — Group Occulting (Oc). A number of occults within a certain time period: Oc (3).

Isophase — Isophase (Iso). The periods of light and dark are equal.

Morse — Morse (Mo (A)). Shows a morse letter (in this case 'A').

Fig 9.11 Light characteristics

Leading lines

One of the most helpful guides to entering or leaving an unfamiliar harbour are leading lines. They consist of two readily identifiable marks (or lights at night) which, when kept in line or in transit, indicate the direction of the safe water channel or harbour entrance, Plate 3. Make a note from the chart of the direction (or bearing) of the transit line: sometimes it is difficult to identify one of the transit marks or lights and knowing where to look relative to the other is important.

Transits

To keep two objects in line or in transit does not require them to be designated as a leading line. Any two objects identifiable on a chart can be used to indicate a desired direction or bearing, Plate 17. In open water a good way to compensate for a crossing tidal stream (a cross tide) is to keep the destination, which may well be a buoy, in transit with any fixed point on the coastline. The use of a transit on the approach to an anchorage is recommended, Fig 9.12.

Clearing bearings

Underwater hazards or dangers are not always marked by buoys or beacons. In the approaches to a harbour there is usually an

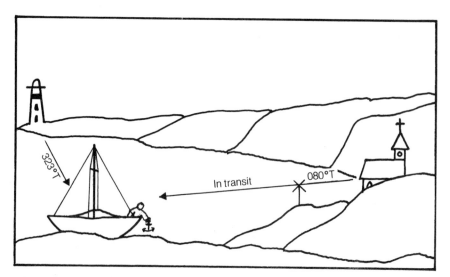

Fig 9.12 Boat anchors when the beacon and the church are in transit and the lighthouse bears 323°T

identifiable landmark in the locality. From the chart a line from this landmark passing clear of the hazard is determined. The direction of this line, represented as a bearing of the landmark, is known as a **clearing bearing**. From safe water if this bearing is not crossed, then the boat will not be in danger from the hazard, Fig 9.13.

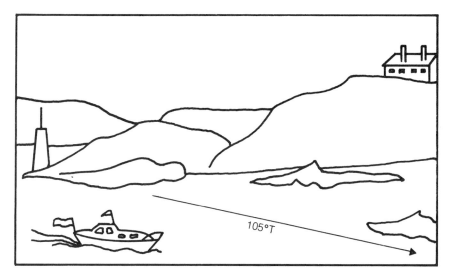

Fig 9.13 A clearing bearing. Provided the beacon bears more than 105°T the boat is in safe water

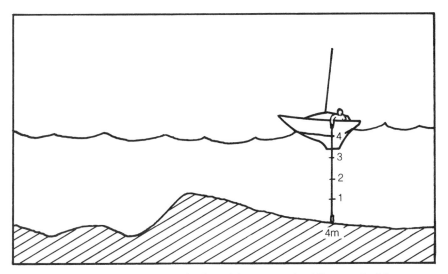

Fig 9.14 The depth of water can be found by using a lead line marked in metres

Depth contours

The depth of water in the boat's present position is measured using an instrument known as a depth-sounder or echo-sounder, or by using a lead line (a heavy weight on the end of a line knotted at one metre intervals), Fig 9.14.

A line joining points on the seabed of equal depth is known as a **depth contour**. In areas where these contours are fairly straight they can be used either as a position line or as an indication of the edge of a channel, Fig 9.15.

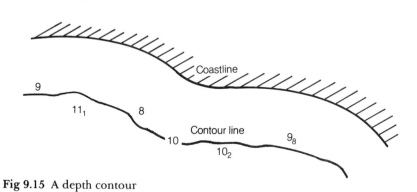

Fig 9.15 A depth contour

QUESTIONS

9.1a. Describe Anvil Point light:
i. by day   ii. by night
   b.   Approaching the light at night, at what distance, approximately, would it first be seen? (Assume a height of eye of 2m and that it is high water.)
   c.   How would you recognise the lighthouse in fog?

9.2   In a position 50° 37′.2N 1° 54′.7W, is it possible to use Anvil Point lighthouse for a bearing? What other landmarks are suitable for a bearing?

9.3   A boat is in estimated position 50° 40′.2N 1° 55′.0W. The original plan had been to locate East Hook buoy and then enter Poole harbour via the inshore passage; but there was a delay due to a fouled anchor and it is now dark. The navigator sights a green light occulting every 6 seconds on a bearing of 320°M and a white light showing a long flash every 10 seconds in transit with a flashing yellow light on a bearing of 181°M. Assuming that the tide is approaching high water, should he enter Poole harbour via the inshore passage; and if so describe the sequence of the passage as far as the main channel.

9.4   When approaching Poole entrance, a boat sees the chain ferry hoist a black ball on its seaward side. What does this indicate; and what action should a boat take?

9.5a.   A boat in an estimated position 50° 35'.5N 1° 57'.0W is making for the anchorage off Swanage. The tidal stream is north-going. It is dark but the visibility is good. How can she keep clear of Peveril Ledge?

   b.   How can she identify Swanage pier by night?

Chapter Ten

Where Have We Been?

Estimated position

We have until now been using the chart for pilotage where we have known our position in relation to the navigational marks. However we will not always be in sight of such marks so, to keep a record of our progress, we estimate our position by recording the boat's

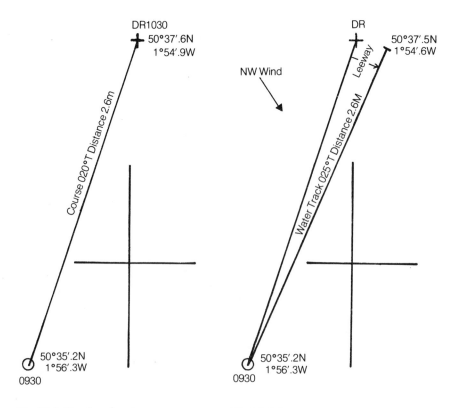

Fig 10.1 Dead reckoning   **Fig 10.2** Leeway

course and distance run together with estimated tidal streams and leeway (the sideways movement caused by the wind).

Let us assume that it is 0930 and we are in a position 50° 35'.2N 1° 56'.3W. From this position we steer a course of 020°T for a distance of 2.6M over a period of one hour. With no allowance for tidal stream or leeway, our 1030 position would be 50° 37'.6N 1° 54'.9W. This is a **dead reckoning (DR)** position, Fig 10.1, and is shown on the chart by using the symbol +.

(*Note:* Normally distances and speeds are rounded up to the nearest tenth of a mile or tenth of a knot. The large scale of chart 15 sometimes makes this difficult.)

However a north west wind has pushed the boat off course through an angle of 5° so that the track of the boat through the water is 025°T. This sideways displacement is known as **leeway**. The track of the boat through the water is known as **water track**. Allowing for this leeway, the 1030 position is 50° 37'.5N 1° 54'.6W. In practice it is the water track which is plotted on the chart, not the true course, Fig 10.2.

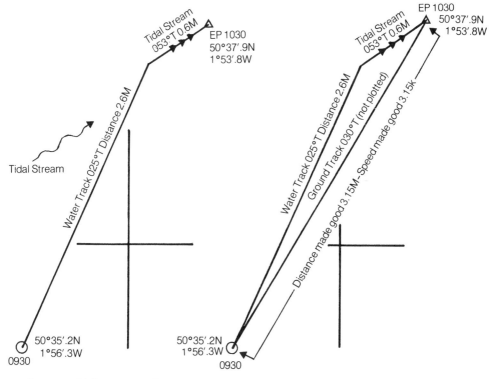

Fig 10.3 Tidal stream and estimated position

Fig 10.4 Ground track distance and speed made good

There is also a tidal stream setting towards the direction 053°T at a rate of 0.6 knots. A **knot** is the equivalent of one nautical mile per hour, and is usually indicated by the suffix 'k' or 'kn'. We must allow for this tidal stream. We plot it from the end of the water track, Fig 10.3.

The resultant position at 1030 now takes into account both leeway and tidal stream. It is known as an **estimated position** (**EP**) and is marked on the chart with the symbol △ . The EP is 50° 37'.9N 1° 53'.8W.

In the example the boat's speed was 2.6k (2.6M in one hour). The line drawn from the 0930 fix to the 1030 EP is known as the **ground track** and represents the effective track of the boat over the land (as opposed to through the water), Fig 10.4. The distance along the ground track from the 0930 fix to the 1030 EP is the **distance made good over the ground** or just **distance made good** (**DMG**). In this example the distance made good is 3.15M (rounded to 3.2M). The **speed made good** (**SMG**) is the distance made good over a period of one hour; which, in this example, is 3.15 (3.2)k. Do not confuse the boat's speed through the water (2.6k) with her speed made good over the ground (3.2k). (*Note:* The ground track is not normally plotted.)

Estimated positions are usually plotted at hourly intervals; but may be plotted for any period of time. In the above example let us find the EP at 1000; which represents a time period of 30 minutes. The water track is still 025° but the distance run is 1.3M (which is the distance travelled at a speed of 2.6k for 30 minutes). The tidal stream is still 053° but the **drift** (distance that the water moves relative to the ground) is 0.3M (0.6k for 30 minutes). We now have the 1000 estimated position and can measure the distance made good between 0930 and 1000 which is 1.6M, Fig 10.5. Note that the speed made good is equivalent to the distance made good divided by the time (in hours): in this example it is still 3.2k.

The triangle formed by the water track, the tidal stream and the ground track is known as a **vector triangle**.

For a passage of several hours the estimated position can be derived by plotting the DR position for the passage then including all the tidal streams consecutively, Fig 10.6. Note that the resultant ground track only represents the mean of the course and tidal streams over the *duration* of the passage.

Time to tack

If a sailing boat is beating to windward, she may wish to know the time at which to tack in order to reach her destination. Firstly determine the best course that the helmsman can steer on each tack and

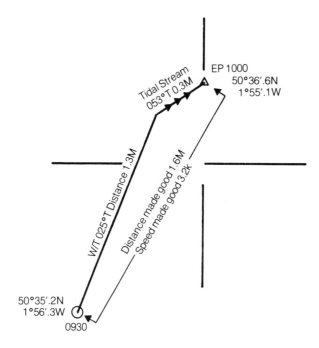

Fig 10.5 A half-hour vector

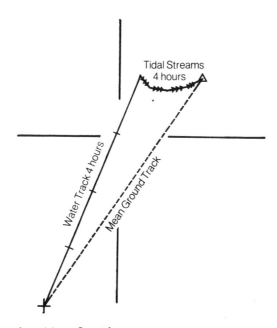

Fig 10.6 Estimated position after 4 hours

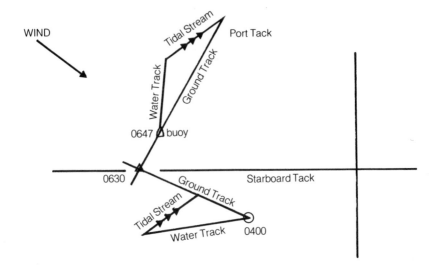

Fig 10.7 Time to tack

then convert these two courses to water tracks. The better tack with which to start is that which keeps the boat's ground track nearest to the direct course to the destination. From the starting point draw on the chart the ground track for the next hour (or half hour if the distance to go is small), Fig 10.7. Estimate roughly the time to tack and the approximate duration of the passage on the second tack. For the period of this duration (rounded to the nearest hour or half hour) draw on the chart *from the destination* the ground track for the second tack. (Note that this is only a construction so it does not matter where the lines go.) Project backwards this ground track to intersect the ground track of the first tack. The point of intersection of the two ground tracks is the position of the change of tack. Measure the distance and speed made good along each track and work out the **time to tack** and the **ETA** (estimated time of arrival) at the destination.

QUESTIONS

Use chart 15 and variation 5°W

10.1 At 1215, log 22.4, a motor boat steering a course of 019°M is in a position 50° 35′.5N 1° 54′.5W. The tidal stream is 053°T 0.8k. At 1245 the log reads 24.3M.

    a. Plot the DR position at 1245.
    b. Plot the EP at 1245.
    c. What is the direction of the ground track?
    d. What is the speed made good?

10.2 At 0430 a boat sailing at 5k on a course of 355°M is in position 50° 36'.7N 1° 48'.6W. At 0500 she tacks on to a course of 095°M. Leeway is negligible. The tidal stream is 057°T 1.0k. Plot the EP at 0530.

10.3 At 0830, log 20.9, a boat fixes her position as 086°T from Swanage pierhead 1.5M. She steers a course of 006°M. At 0900, log 22.6, she arrives at Poole Fairway buoy. What has been the direction and rate of the tidal stream between 0830 and 0900?

10.4 At 1150 a boat, sailing a course of 051°M at a speed of 4.0k, is in a position 50° 35'.5N 1° 55'.5W. Leeway is 10° due to a north wind. At 1250 she tacks to a course of 320°M. HW Portsmouth is at 1720 BST; it is neaps. Plot the EPs at 1250 and 1320. Use tidal diamond A for the first hour and tidal diamond B thereafter.

10.5 The following is an extract from the log of a boat on passage from Christchurch to Poole:

Time		Log	Course	Dev	Wind	Leeway
1600	Position 159°T CG Lookout 0.5M Sounding 12.8m	1.3	286°C	3°W	N6	5°
1700	Bournemouth pierhead bears 297°M Altered course to 233°C	5.4	233°C	2°W	N5	Nil
1703	Yellow buoy close abeam to starboard	5.6	233°C	2°W	N5	Nil
1749	Red buoy 0.2M on port beam. Engine started. Altered course to 312°C	8.3	312°C	4°W	N5	Nil

Tidal stream between 1600 and 1700: 275°T 0.2k
Tidal stream between 1700 and 1800: Negligible

Plot the EPs at 1700 and 1749. Identify the red buoy abeam at 1749.

Chapter Eleven

Finding Our Position

Position lines

In the last chapter we found out how to estimate our position in the absence of suitable navigational marks. Whereas it is essential to keep a record throughout a passage of the estimated position, accurate positions should be plotted where possible using bearings of suitable land and sea marks which can be identified both visually and on the chart.

We normally use the hand-bearing compass to take the bearings to fix our position. Referring to the south west corner of chart 15 and assuming we are in a DR position (approximate) of 50° 35'.2N 1° 55'.5W, we take these bearings:

Anvil Point lighthouse	299°M
Durlston Head	321°M
Peveril Point	358°M

We will plot these bearings using the protractor scale on the parallel rule. First we convert the magnetic bearings to true bearings allowing for the local variation which is 5°W:

Anvil Point lighthouse	294°T
Durlston Head	316°T
Peveril Point	353°T

Place the rule across the meridian nearest to Anvil Point lighthouse so that it passes through the south point of the protractor scale and the bearing of 294°. Both edges of the rule now lie along the direction of the bearing (and its reciprocal). It may be possible to line up the rule so that an edge also passes through Anvil Point lighthouse, but, if not, we will need to walk the rule so that an edge passes through the lighthouse. Draw a line from the lighthouse in the opposite direction to the bearing: this line is called a **position line** and will have an arrowhead on the end furthest from the lighthouse.

In practice only that part of the position line in the vicinity of the DR position is drawn. We know that our position is somewhere along this position line. A second position line which crosses the first will give our exact position at the point of intersection. To verify the accuracy a third position line (from a bearing taken at the same time) should pass through the same point.

But looking at Fig 11.1 the three position lines do not intersect at a common point but form a triangle (known as a **cocked hat**). The variation has been correctly applied. The error is due to incorrect identification of Durlston Head because of its 'end on' aspect. There is a prominent castle on Durlston Head which makes a better landmark. The bearing of the castle is 320°M or 315°T which gives a much better fix, Fig 11.2.

In practice if three bearings are taken to give three position lines, it is quite likely that a small cocked hat will result particularly if the boat is moving fast or if there is a rough sea. Provided there are no immediate hazards the centre of a small cocked hat is acceptable as the boat's position. If there is a hazard on the course ahead, assume a position at the corner of the cocked hat nearest the hazard. A large cocked hat may be caused by applying the variation in the wrong sense; but if that is not the case the bearings should be taken again. Ideally two position lines should cross at right angles and three position lines should have a relative difference of 60°. Avoid the tempta-

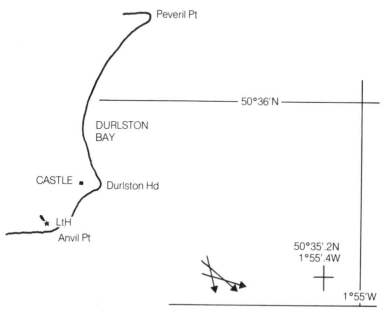

Fig 11.1 A cocked hat

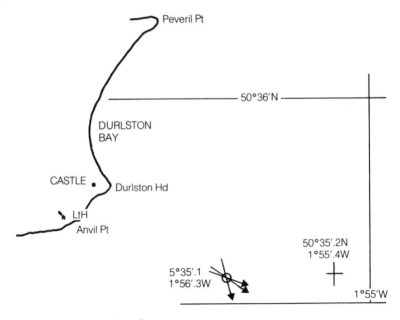

Fig 11.2 Three position line fix

tion to take bearings of objects at great distances particularly if there
are others nearby. Buoys can be out of position so land based
objects are preferred. A position obtained from two or more bearings of landmarks (or buoys) is known as a fix and is indicated on a
chart using the symbol ⊙ . Any position on a chart *must* have the
time marked beside it; and it is also desirable to make a note of the
log reading (in the form of distance travelled).

   Other considerations when taking bearings are:

1. Nearer objects are preferred to distant ones as angular differences will cause smaller errors.
2. Bearings ahead and astern should be taken first as bearings
   abeam alter more rapidly.
3. The use of left or right hand edges of headlands is acceptable
   provided they are steep.
4. Off-lying features may merge with the background and be difficult to locate.
5. Spot heights are useful for identifying sections of a coastline but
   they are no good for bearings as the highest point on the chart
   may not in fact be visible from the boat.
6. At night lights must be positively identified from their characteristics. Car headlights or fishing boats bobbing up and down on
   the waves sometimes give the appearance of the lights of a lighthouse or buoy.

Transferred position line or Running fix

If at any moment we obtain a bearing of a single landmark and sometime later we obtain another single bearing, provided these bearings are different by around 90° we can determine our position.

For example, refer to Fig 11.3. At 1145 Peveril Point bears 352°T. The boat continues on a course of 020°T at a speed of 2.6k with a north west wind causing 5° of leeway. The tidal stream is 053°T 0.6k. At 1215 Peveril Point bears 265°T.

The 1145 position line is plotted on the chart. From *any* point on this line (but normally the closest point to the 1145 DR position) the water track (025°T) is plotted for the distance travelled between 1145 and 1215 (1.3M). For the same time period the tidal stream (053°T 0.3M) is added. The point obtained is an EP relative to the starting point on the 1145 position line. The second position line taken at 1215 is plotted. The first position line is now transferred to pass through the EP and to cross the second position line. The point of intersection is the 1215 position. This method of obtaining a fix is known as a **running fix** or a **transferred position line**. The accuracy

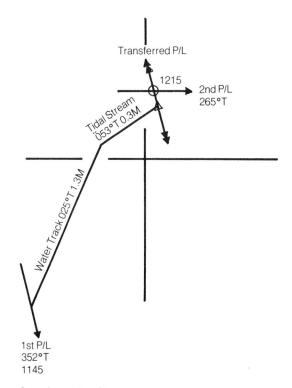

Fig 11.3 Transferred position line

of a running fix depends on the assessment of the boat's course and
speed, the leeway, and the tidal stream. It is not as good a fix as one
obtained from two or more bearings taken at the same time.

Radiobeacons

A marine radiobeacon is marked on the chart with the (magenta)
symbol: ⊙ RC . There is one on the Haven Hotel in position
50° 41'N 1° 57'W. An aeronautical radiobeacon is marked on the
chart with the symbol: ⊙ Aero RC .

A **radio direction finder** or **RDF** is used to identify and obtain a
bearing of a radiobeacon provided it is within range. This bearing
can then be used as a position line for a fix.

Yachtsman's almanacs contain a list of radiobeacons showing
their position, frequency, identity signal, transmission time and
range. Marine radiobeacons normally transmit within a period of a
minute the identity signal (repeated several times), a continuous
tone, and then the identity signal again. With the radio direction
finder tuned to the correct frequency, the radiobeacon is first
identified, then the antenna is rotated in the horizontal plane during the period of continuous tone until the signal level drops to a
minimum (known as a 'null'). From the magnetic compass on the
antenna the bearing is read at the instant of the null. Whilst the bearings of radiobeacons are being taken, the helmsman must be
encouraged to steer a steady course.

There is a null both when the antenna is directly towards the
radiobeacon and when it is pointing directly away. It is usually quite
evident which is correct if the radiobeacon is on the coastline. For a
radiobeacon on an island or lightship, set a course temporarily at
right angles to the bearing of the radiobeacon: if the bearing
increases the radiobeacon is on the starboard side; if it decreases the
radiobeacon is to port.

An aeronautical radiobeacon transmits the continuous tone with
the identity signals superimposed and without any breaks.

The radio beam is refracted (bent) when it passes either from land
to sea or at a narrow angle to the coast so any bearings obtained may
be unreliable. Radio distortion frequently occurs at the time of dusk
and dawn. It is not easy without practice to obtain a good bearing of
a radiobeacon.

Line of soundings

An echo-sounder is an instrument used to measure the depth of
water. (The depth measured is actually between the seabed and the
sensor or transducer mounted on the boat's hull.) The depth of

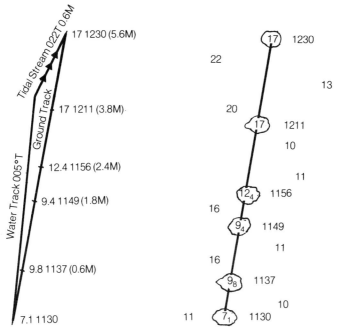

A tidal vector for one hour is plotted to find the ground track

The ground track marked at intervals with soundings is transferred to paper, placed on the chart and moved until it coincides

Fig 11.4 Running a line of soundings

water when corrected for the height of tide corresponds with the depths shown on the chart (called **soundings**). If a boat crossing a shelving seabed records corrected depths at regular time intervals or regular distances from the log readings, a **line of soundings** is obtained, Fig 11.4.

This line of soundings is marked on a strip of paper which can be placed alongside the ground track on the chart and moved forwards or backwards to obtain a correlation with the depths shown on the chart.

If the depth contours (usually 5m, 10m, 15m) on the chart are regular (fairly straight lines), they can be used as underwater position lines. By following a depth contour (altering course to remain in a constant depth of water) it is frequently possible to skirt round an underwater hazard in conditions of poor visibility (see Depth contours: Chapter 9).

Comparison of methods to determine position

1. Two or more visual bearings: very accurate provided that there is a good angle of cut between the position lines.
2. Two or more radio bearings: difficult except where suitable radiobeacons are available.
3. Transferred position line: only as accurate as the assessment of water track, distance run and tidal stream.
4. Line of soundings: the approximate position of the boat must be known and there must be distinguishable features on the seabed.
5. Estimated position: the best estimate of the boat's position taking into account the accuracies of the course steered, the distance run, the leeway and the direction and rate of the tidal stream.
6. Dead reckoning: the position obtained *only* from the course steered and distance run.

(*Note:* Close inshore, there may not be time to fix the boat's position. A leading line allows a rapid appreciation of any tendency for the boat to be set off track. Clearing bearings help ensure that navigational hazards are avoided. An echo-sounder should always be used for verification of position.)

QUESTIONS

Use chart 15 and variation 5°W

11.1　At 1400 a motor boat in an estimated position 50° 35′.4N 1° 57′.2W takes the following bearings using the hand-bearing compass:

Anvil Point lighthouse	345°M
Castle on Durlston Head	040°M

　a. Plot fix.

　b. As only two bearings were available, what could be done to check the accuracy of the fix?

　c. Assuming the log is accurate, what may account for the difference between the EP and the fix?

11.2　The same boat continues on a course of 263°C. At 1420 she sights two beacons in transit. The bearing of these beacons on the steering compass is 355°C and on the hand-bearing compass 359°M.

　a. What is the deviation of the steering compass?

　b. Can this deviation be used for any heading of the boat?

　c. Is there any deviation on the hand-bearing compass?

　d. Can the hand-bearing compass be assumed to have any deviation?

11.3   At 1130, log 3.8, a boat, steering a course of 014°M, is in a DR position 50° 35′.2N 1° 55′.4W. She takes a bearing of Anvil Point lighthouse: 284°M.

At 1200, log 5.7, the right-hand edge of Handfast Point bears 353°M. The west wind is causing 5° of leeway. The tidal stream between 1130 and 1230 is 049°T 1.0k.

   a. Plot the position at 1200.

   b. What is the accuracy of the 1200 position?

   c. How would you write this position as a direction and distance from Handfast Point?

11.4   At 0930 a boat in DR position 50° 42′.5N 1° 51′.0W takes the following bearings using a hand-bearing compass:

Bournemouth Pier	286°M
Boscombe Pier	052°M
Conspicuous hotel in Bournemouth (right hand edge)	005°M
Yellow buoy (off Bournemouth Pier)	267°M

   a. Plot fix.

   b. What comments can you make about the bearings?

11.5   At 0915 on a course of 094°M a boat takes a bearing of the CG Lookout on Hengistbury Head: 050°M. At the same time the echo-sounder reads 11.0m. The height of tide is estimated as 0.8m. The boat's draught is 2.0m and the transducer of the echo-sounder is 0.3m below the waterline.

   a. Is this a positive fix?

   b. Should the boat take any action?

Chapter Twelve

How To Get There

Course to steer

We need to know our present position both to be sure that we are clear of any hazards and to determine the direction and distance to the next point on our way or passage (a **waypoint**). On a large scale chart (such as chart 15) we can draw in the desired ground track from waypoint to waypoint and then check our position at regular intervals to ensure that we are close enough to the track and clear of any potential dangers. For longer passages and in poor visibility we must be able to work out the course to steer to the next waypoint compensating for the tidal stream, leeway, variation and deviation with the same degree of accuracy that we required for working out our estimated position (see Chapter 10).

Referring to chart 15, let us assume that at 0900 we are in position 50° 35'.9N 1° 52'.5W and we want to know the course to steer to Poole Fairway buoy in position 50° 39'.0N 1° 54'.8W. We first draw a line from our 0900 position to the buoy. This line represents our desired ground track, Fig 12.1.

The distance along the ground track is 3.4M. If we were able to sail directly along the ground track with no leeway or tidal stream, at a speed of 4k we would reach the buoy in 51 minutes at 0951.

$$\frac{3.4}{4} \times 60 = 51 \text{ minutes: that is } 0951.$$

If there was a tidal stream setting towards 046°T at 1.3k we make allowances in the following manner. The time to reach the buoy will be (as an initial rough estimate) about one hour, so we will use one hour's worth of tidal stream: 046°T 1.3M. The tidal stream is drawn *from the 0900 position*, Fig 12.2.

In one hour the boat will have travelled through the water a distance of 4.0M. Using the dividers measure a distance of 4.0M on the latitude scale. With one point of the dividers on the end of the tidal stream vector, place the other point of the dividers on the ground

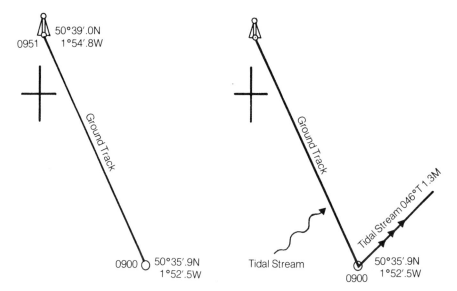

Fig 12.1 Ground track

Fig 12.2 Tidal stream

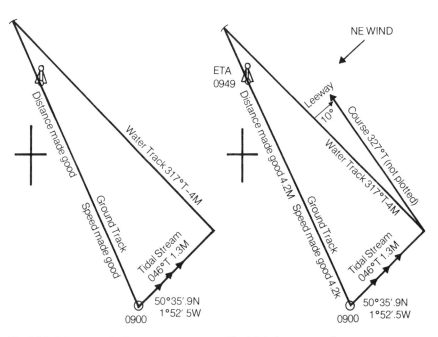

Fig 12.3 Water track distance and speed made good

Fig 12.4 Leeway and true course

track (extending the ground track if necessary) and mark this position. The line from the end of the tidal stream vector to this position is the water track. The position marked will be the estimated position *after one hour*, that is at 1000, Fig 12.3. We now measure the direction of the water track: 317°T.

In order that the water track can be converted to the correct course to steer to achieve the desired ground track, we have to compensate for any leeway by steering into the wind: *towards* the direction from which the wind is blowing. If there was a wind from the north east causing 10° of leeway, we would need to steer a course of 327°T, Fig 12.4.

The **course to steer** is the course given to the helmsman, so it must include corrections for compass variation and (if necessary) deviation. With a variation of 5°W and zero deviation, our course to steer is 332°C.

The speed made good is the distance made good for a period of one hour as measured along the ground track between the positions at 0900 and 1000. It is 4.2k (Fig 12.4).

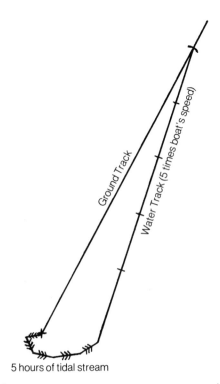

5 hours of tidal stream

Fig 12.5 Plotting 5-hour vector

We may need to know our **Estimated Time of Arrival** or **ETA** at the buoy. The 1000 estimated position is beyond the buoy so we will take less than one hour to reach the buoy. From the 0900 position the distance to the buoy, measured along the ground track, is 3.4M. The speed made good is 4.2k. The time taken to reach the buoy is 49 minutes.

$$\frac{3.4}{4.2} \times 60 = 49 \text{ minutes.}$$

So the ETA at the Poole Fairway buoy is 0949.

There is no need to use a period of one hour. For instance on a large scale chart a half-hour period may be more suitable. The distances drawn would correspond to half an hour of tidal stream and half an hour of boat speed giving the distance made good in half an hour (so speed made good would be twice the distance made good). For a long passage of 5 hours the tidal streams over that period are aggregated together from the starting point; a distance of 5 times the boat's speed is drawn from the tidal stream vectors to the ground track, this line being the water track and the point of intersection

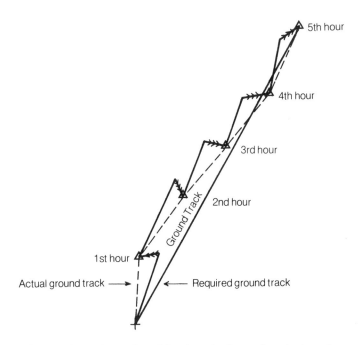

Fig 12.6 Plotting the estimated position hourly shows that the boat is near the required ground track but not on it until the fifth hour

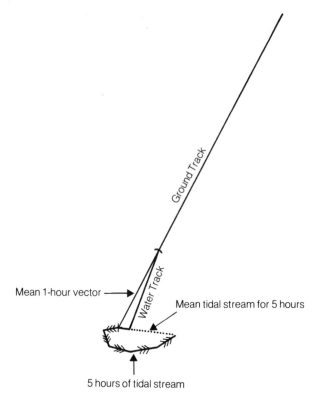

Fig 12.7 Plotting a one-hour vector using the mean tidal stream for 5 hours

with the ground track being the estimated position for a time 5 hours after the start, Fig 12.5. In this case, whilst we can make a reasonable estimate of the course to steer (from the water track), the boat may well not be on the ground track until the end of the passage, Fig 12.6. An alternative is to determine the mean tidal stream over a period of time and apply it on an hourly basis, Fig 12.7.

QUESTIONS

Use chart 15 and variation 5°W

12.1   A boat at Poole Fairway buoy wishes to make good a ground track of 060°T. Her speed is 4.0k. The tidal stream is 344°T 0.7k. Wind SE. Leeway 10°. What is the magnetic course to steer?

12.2   A boat at Boscombe Pier at 1750 BST is heading towards Poole Fairway buoy at a speed of 4.0k. What is the magnetic course to steer? What is her ETA? Use tidal diamond B; HW Portsmouth 1420, springs. Wind NE5, leeway 5°.

12.3 At 1550 a boat is in a position 50° 37'.0N 1° 49'.5W. What is the magnetic course to steer at a speed of 2.5k to Poole Fairway buoy? Use tidal diamond A for the first hour and tidal diamond B for the remainder. Wind S, leeway 10°. HW Portsmouth 1923, neaps. What is the ETA at the buoy?

12.4 At 1150 a boat is in a position 50° 35'.4N 1° 55'.5W. Wind N, leeway 10°. At a speed of 3k, she needs to make good a ground track of 050°T. Use tidal diamond A for first hour; then tidal diamond B. HW Portsmouth 1720; neaps. She tacks at 1250. What is the magnetic course to Poole Fairway buoy and what is the ETA?

12.5 At 0900 BST a motor boat is in a position 095°T Anvil Point lighthouse 1.5M. What is the magnetic course to steer to the position 084°T Old Harry rock 1.0M? Leeway nil. Speed 6k. HW Portsmouth 1515; springs. Use tidal diamond B.

Chapter Thirteen

What Part Does the Weather Play?

Mist and fog

From the point of view of the navigator, one of the worst hazards at sea is poor visibility. All the visual landmarks have disappeared! Electronic aids to navigation become very much more desirable and should be constantly monitored where available. However, the cardinal rule is to plot meticulously at regular intervals the dead reckoning and estimated positions. If fog is forecast make regular fixes until the landmarks are no longer visible. Try and maintain a steady course. A reliable means of measuring distance run is essential, so the log (the instrument for measuring distance travelled through the water) must be trustworthy. Whilst it may be relatively straightforward to avoid underwater hazards, the principal hazard in poor visibility is other shipping.

If the visibility is less than 5M it is said to be moderate; and if it is less than 2M it is poor. Mist (water droplets) and haze (dust particles) give a visibility which is defined as 2M or less. Visibility in fog is less than 0.5M; and in thick fog less than 0.25M. If poor visibility is forecast, then it is prudent to be prepared to abandon the passage for an alternative destination that can be reached before the visibility deteriorates. It may be sensible to anchor close inshore until the fog clears.

However suppose we set out on a clear sunny day not expecting any changes. The horizon has become indistinct; the fishing boat that we have just passed is becoming blurred; the sun's rays seem less warming: definite signs of an approaching fog-bank. What actions should we take?

1. *Get a fix.* Try to get a fix of the boat's position by any means available. Record the time and log reading. If this is not possible, then work out the estimated position from the last known position. Draw on the chart the anticipated course and DR positions for

the next few hours. Check the availability of radio navigation aids. Switch on the echo-sounder and navigation lights.

2. *Note positions and direction of travel of any other shipping* particularly any vessels that might pass close by.

3. *Take safety precautions.* Hoist radar reflector (if not permanently fitted); check fog signalling apparatus; don lifejackets; if carried, check that the liferaft is ready to launch; if there is no liferaft inflate the dinghy and tow it astern; if under sail, check that the engine is ready to start immediately; post a look-out in the bows; maintain silence on deck; brief all crew on deck to listen for fog signals from other vessels.
   (*Note:* One of the main hazards in poor visibility is the risk of collision.)

4. *Review the passage plan.* Should the course to the present destination be maintained; would it be prudent to anchor in shallow water until visibility improves, or would it be safer to go out to sea.

5. If following a buoyed channel, *make a list of the buoys with their characteristics and note the direction and distance from each buoy to the next.* Tick off buoys as they are passed comparing with distance the elapsed time between them. Use the echo-sounder to keep within the channel and remember at all times which side of the boat the safe (deeper) water lies.

6. *When approaching a harbour* clear of any outlying dangers, it is a good plan to *set a course towards one side of the entrance.* Then, when the shoreline is sighted or a particular depth contour reached, there is no doubt which way to alter course for the harbour entrance. If there is a strong tidal stream across the entrance, set a course well upstream so that the tidal stream will be fair (favourable) when the shoreline is sighted.

7. *Listen for the fog signals of lighthouses.* Note that it is not easy to determine the direction of sounds in foggy conditions. If the lighthouse is fitted with a marine radiobeacon, then using a Radio Direction Finder (RDF) to maintain the radiobeacon on a constant bearing simplifies locating the harbour entrance.

Strong winds

Settled weather or stable weather conditions are ideal for cruising in small boats. There can be strong winds in these conditions but their strength and direction is usually consistent. Associated weather forecasts usually mention 'high pressure zones', 'anti-cyclones' and 'slow moving'.

Unsettled weather is caused by areas of low pressure (depressions) and associated frontal troughs (fronts). This brings clouds and rain;

but particularly winds that can vary rapidly in both strength and direction. Knowledge of the movement of these depressions and fronts does enable the weather to be predicted; and these predictions for a period 24 hours ahead are regularly broadcast or published.

For a small boat of length less than 9 metres a wind of strength (force) 6, which is a wind speed of about 25 knots, is normally the limit of comfortable sailing. A larger boat may be able to cope with gale force 8 (35 knots). The Beaufort Wind Scale is shown on the back of chart 15.

Running downwind is more comfortable than beating to windward. However, it is the combination of wind and sea-state that affect the ability of a sailing boat to make a safe passage in strong winds. If the wind is blowing in the opposite direction to the tidal stream, the sea may become very rough particularly at spring tides. Under these conditions shallow water, tide races and overfalls can become dangerous even though the charted depth may be adequate. In open seas a wave pattern can build up which is not particularly hazardous in itself but if the wind changes another wave pattern can be superimposed on the original which causes very rough seas. This effect can also occur near (within a half mile) of a sea wall where the reflected wave is superimposed on the original.

Provided a boat is well constructed and equipped, the sails are reefed, and the crew are not prone to seasickness, then strong winds need be no deterrent to the completion of a passage provided sensible precautions are observed. More prudence may be required before setting off on a long passage with a forecast of strong winds.

With strong winds forecast, the following precautions should be observed:

1. Most emergencies in rough weather are caused by the failure of the crew rather than the boat. Tiredness, cold and hunger increase the likelihood of seasickness. If an extended sea passage is anticipated, let any crew not required go below to rest. Wind chill cools quicker than most people realise, so extra warm clothes must be put on early before shivering starts. A substantial hot meal before a night passage and at breakfast time is desirable; and frequent light snacks and drinks should be encouraged. If necessary make a large box of sandwiches. Above all, seasickness tablets must be taken well in advance; not just as the motion starts to deteriorate.

2. In a small boat it is very difficult to navigate in rough weather. Often the deck log is not kept up to date: with no log readings and course alterations recorded, it is impossible to estimate a position. Usually it is not easy to remain at the chart table for pro-

longed periods without feeling queasy. The solution is careful preparation. The charts should be stowed accessibly in the order that they will be required. All tidal information should be extracted from the almanac and recorded in a 'navigator's note-book'. On the tidal stream atlas or diagram, fill in the time of high water and the hours before and after high water. For all har-bours along the route of the passage key information should be noted: direction of tidal streams in the approach; conspicuous landmarks; characteristics of lights and buoys; details of clearing bearings and transits. Each chart should be marked up with the route including the compass course for each change of direction; together with highlighting of all hazards and conspicuous land-marks, clearing bearings, and change-over positions from one chart to the next.

3. Secure the boat for sea. In a rough sea everything that can move will move. Keeping accessible those items that may be required, lash down or secure everything else so that it cannot shift about. Check all hatches are secure. The anchor may be better lashed inboard rather than over the bow.

4. Reef the sails early; it is much easier to increase sail if the wind drops than to shorten sail if the wind increases. When the wind increases enough for sails to be reefed all the crew on deck and in the cockpit should be wearing safety harnesses and clip on to the safety lines or strong points. Do not use guardrails for securing safety harnesses: they are not strong enough to take the snatch load of a person falling overboard.

5. If it is decided to anchor (or remain in an anchorage) more anchor cable is necessary in strong winds. In fair weather if the anchor cable is all chain, then the simple rule is *3 × maximum depth of water*; if the cable is a short length (6m) of chain backed by a nylon warp, then let out *5 × maximum depth of water*. In strong winds let out *8 × maximum depth of water*; and, if possible, let go a second anchor.

Lee shore

For hundreds of years seafaring yarns have recounted the hazards of a lee shore. If there is a shoreline on the leeward side of the boat (as opposed to the windward side) it is called a **lee shore**. It is a shore-line on to which the wind is blowing. A powerless vessel will be blown by the wind on to a lee shore. If the seabed gradually shelves upwards to the shore, then in strong onshore winds the waves will build up into breakers which will crash down on the coastline. Any vessel caught up in these breakers has little chance of survival. Any harbour with its entrance or approach open to windward becomes extremely hazardous in strong winds. A small craft at sea should keep clear of a lee shore in heavy weather and should not contemplate entering such a harbour. Not a happy decision for the skipper of a small boat with nightfall approaching and with a tired, cold and seasick crew.

Weather forecasts

To avoid some of the problems of poor visibility and strong winds, careful attention should be paid to weather forecasts. The sources can be summarised as follows:

1. *Shipping forecasts.* These are broadcast on BBC Radio 4 (long wave) at 0033, 0555, 1355 and 1750. BBC Radio 4 has a wavelength of 1500 metres which is equivalent to a frequency of 200 kilohertz (200 kHz). The forecast lists any gale warnings in force, gives a general synopsis of the weather patterns affecting the UK Continental Shelf, forecasts the weather over the next 24 hours for the sea areas surrounding the United Kingdom and gives details of the weather reported at coastal weather stations. While much of the detail may not be relevant, it is a most useful forecast for a small boat sailor contemplating a coastal passage.

2. *Inshore waters forecast.* This is broadcast on BBC Radio 4 after the shipping forecast at 0033 and on BBC Radio 3 at 0655. It is a forecast of the weather expected around the UK coastline (within 12 miles of the coast) for the next 24 hours. Winds along the coastline are normally not as strong as in the open sea; but occasionally in local areas funnelling can cause stronger winds.

3. *Local radio forecasts.* Local radio stations broadcast weather reports and forecasts some of which specifically cover the requirements of sailing enthusiasts. The information is up to date and specific for a locality. Frequently additional information such as times of local high tides, shipping movements, and navigational warnings are included. Land weather forecasts contain much useful supplementary information.

4. *Newspapers and television.* The synoptic charts in newspapers and on television are particularly useful for observing long term trends in weather patterns in anticipation of a weekend sail or a cruise lasting several days. The information in newspapers is not up to date.

5. *Marinecall.* A telephone call-in service specially for yachtsmen. Forecasts are given for specific coastal areas and are updated every six hours.

6. *Weather centres.* The London Weather Centre and other local weather centres can be contacted for information on the

weather forecast for periods up to 5 days ahead. A personal visit is better than telephoning.

7. *Coastguard.* The Coastguard broadcast weather information at regular intervals. They will repeat the local forecast if requested on the VHF radio telephone (channel 67). They also broadcast strong wind warnings (Force 6 and above).

8. *Coast radio stations (British Telecom).* Daily at 0803 or 0833 and at 2003 or 2033 (Greenwich Mean Time) Coast Radio Stations re-broadcast the shipping forecast for the local area.

9. *Local air stations.* All air stations have a duty forecaster. If he is not busy he can provide a very good up to date local forecast.

10. *Gale warnings.* On BBC Radio 4 gale warnings received from the Meteorological Office are broadcast at the next programme break after receipt and on completion of the next news bulletin. Gale warnings are also broadcast by the Coastguard and local radio stations in addition to strong winds warnings. A strong wind is Force 6 and above.

Generally record barometer readings and wind strength and direction regularly, preferably hourly, and watch for any changes other than gradual. Watch the clouds: personal experience based on observation is very valuable.

QUESTIONS

See back of chart 15 where appropriate

13.1   A navigator is about to plan a passage. Where can he obtain:
a. the details of present and expected weather including wind direction and strength, visibility and sea state?
b. the position and movement of weather systems likely to affect the passage and details of any gale warnings?

13.2   A navigator missed the shipping forecast at 0555. Where can he obtain the gale warnings, general synopsis, sea area forecast and reports from coast stations for a passage from Yarmouth to Swanage?

13.3   A motor boat is leaving Poole harbour on the ebb tide. The conditions are calm but the visibility is poor and deteriorating. The only landmark in sight is the beacon at the end of the Training Bank which is close to starboard. From dead ahead comes the sound of engines and a prolonged blast on a siren. What action should be taken?

13.4   The wind has been blowing SW 6–7 for the past two days but has now veered to NW 5. The following types of boat propose to leave Poole harbour on the ebb tide at springs to round Anvil Point continuing their passage to westward. How would you expect each boat to react to weather and sea state?

   a. Motor boat, length 10m, shallow draught, cruising speed 8k.

   b. Deep fin-keeled sailing boat, length 12m, cruising speed 7k.

   c. Twin bilge-keeled sailing boat, length 9m, cruising speed 5k.

13.5 What do the following terms mean:

   a. **poor** visibility

   b. a depression moving **rapidly**

   c. a **near gale**

   d. a **moderate breeze**

   e. **later**

Chapter Fourteen

Planning Ahead

Before embarking on any sea passage, whether it is just a trip out of the harbour or a voyage across the English Channel, it is necessary to plan things out well beforehand.

The amount of pre-planning will depend on: the experience of the navigator; the equipment available; knowledge of the area concerned; the locality; the length of the passage.

Here are some of the things to do a day or so before:

1. All charts to be used should be checked to see whether they need updating and the latest *Notices to Mariners* obtained to see that no corrections have been missed. A visit to the Harbour Master's office usually pays dividends as he will have details of any activities or changes within the harbour limits such as dredging or maintenance of navigational marks.

2. A small scale chart is needed initially to plan the voyage. Larger scale charts will be required for coastal passages. The largest scale charts will be required for any harbours or anchorages that may be visited.

3. Look over the sails; check standing and running rigging, safety equipment, wet weather gear, cooking facilities and engine. Check the batteries. Check the dinghy and outboard motor. Ensure that the crew are familiar with the location of safety equipment and emergency procedures.

4. Start a record of the general weather pattern.

5. Work out the starting time for the voyage, taking into consideration tides and daylight hours. Check the tides at the destination bearing in mind the opening times of locks and basins. Measure the mileage, inspect the tidal streams and make a rough estimate of the time to complete the passage allowing for the boat's normal cruising speed. Check times of sunrise and sunset, see Extract 7, p. 123. Fill in the tidal stream atlas. Draw in the pro-

posed track and check for any hazards on the way. If using an electronic position fixing system, mark in the waypoints. Highlight any conspicuous landmarks. For a night passage list the characteristics together with the visibility range and bearing of all lights likely to be encountered (remembering that buoys are not generally visible at a range greater than 2M). Establish alternative destinations in case of unforeseen circumstances.

6. Before the passage fill up with water and fuel and check that a spare gas bottle (for the cooker) is on board. Stow all gear below and secure all items on deck. Get the latest weather forecast. Ensure that a responsible person ashore knows both the details of your passage and who will be on board. As soon as departure time is confirmed work out the DR positions (and estimated positions if time) for the first leg of the passage.

7. As the harbour entrance is cleared, set the log to zero and give the helmsman the course to steer (assuming if under sail that the course to steer is not into wind). As soon as the boat's speed can be established, check the estimated positions for the first part of the passage.

8. If the course to steer is into the wind, it is important to establish from the helmsman the best course he can steer on each tack. When beating to windward (making a series of tacks into wind) the navigator will need to decide when to tack to make best use of any tidal streams and to keep clear of any navigational hazards. In anticipation of any shift in wind direction, keep within 5M of the desired track reducing this distance progressively as the destination or waypoint is approached. (Keep within a cone of 20° from the desired track as measured from the destination.)

9. Fix the boat's position regularly: at least every 30 minutes if within sight of land. Compare the estimated positions and fixes to make allowance for any deviation from the desired track. Record the log reading every hour; and the barometric pressure and wind direction and speed at least every four hours. The deck log should contain sufficient navigational information so that the broad details of the passage could be re-created at a later date.

10. If the weather conditions are deteriorating, be prepared to make for an alternative destination or to turn back.

11. When the ETA (estimated time of arrival) at the destination is established, re-check any restrictions due to tidal stream or height of tide. Be prepared to anchor or pick up a mooring near the entrance. Check for local signals restricting entry to the harbour or any tidal basins.

12. Frequently when entering an unfamiliar harbour it is not clear

where a visitor should go initially. Use of a VHF radio (if available) to call up the local marina or harbour master is ideal. If visitor's moorings or berths can be identified, they should be used. Otherwise it may be necessary to secure to a vacant buoy or pontoon in order that a crew member can proceed ashore to seek advice on berthing. Should the owner return meanwhile, at least he will be able to give guidance on an alternative berth; but be prepared to move at short notice.

Chapter Fifteen

An Extra Crew Member

A position finding system, such as Decca, Loran or a Satellite Navigator, is a valuable aid to navigation. Provided it is working satisfactorily it can give a constant read-out of the boat's present position. Normally the present position is based on a fix from two or three position lines obtained from bearings of landmarks taken with the hand-bearing compass. An electronic system does not require a landmark to be visible.

In all position finding systems the first objective is to establish the boat's position as a latitude and longitude. Additional selected positions, known as waypoints, can be entered and the computer will derive direction and distance from the boat's position to any of these waypoints or between any of the waypoints. Course and speed made good can also be displayed. Man overboard position markers are sometimes included. Some systems will work out tidal stream or current if the boat's course and speed are entered.

In conditions where navigation is difficult, such electronic aids make a significant contribution to safety. If a position fixing system is installed it should be used; but only to supplement the other methods of establishing a boat's position.

Radio and electronic aids

Hyperbolic systems

A hyperbolic system relies on ground transmitters whose accurate position is known. Two transmitters are used to obtain one position line; and two others to obtain a second position line. Where the two lines intersect is the boat's position. The two transmitters are synchronised and the times of arrival of the two transmissions are measured. If the boat is equidistant from the two transmitters, both transmissions will arrive together. If the boat is nearer one transmitter than the other, the nearest transmitter's signal will arrive first. A

96

measurement of the difference in time between the two arrivals will therefore be a measurement of the relative distance of the two transmitters. There will be many points on the surface of the earth where there will be the same difference in time between the arrival of the two signals and, if they were joined together by a line, its shape would be a hyperbola. Having located himself on one hyperbola, the user must locate himself on another in order to get an intersection. He does this by measuring the time difference between the arrival of signals from two other transmitters. However, normally the area is covered by only three transmitters; the main or master station transmits first and triggers off the other two slave stations. They transmit after the master, but since their distance from the master is known, the delay of these transmissions is also known and this is allowed for in the receiving equipment aboard the boat. Two position lines are thus obtained: one between the master and slave A and the other between the master and slave B. The hyperbolic position lines can be drawn on a chart, but it is more usual for an on-board computer to work it all out and present the yachtsman with his position in latitude and longitude.

Decca

The Decca system operates in coastal waters around north-west Europe and in other local areas around the world. The effective range is 300M but this can diminish during night hours. Because of its limited range it is not suitable for ocean passage making. The accuracy is about 50m within 50M of the transmitters. The sets originally leased by Racal Decca Marine were used in conjunction with charts with a Decca lattice overlaid on them. It was relatively easy to see that where the lattice was compact the accuracy was high and as distance from the transmitter was increased the lattice pattern opened up with a consequent decrease in potential accuracy. On the base line from a master station extended beyond a slave station the lattice was very indeterminate which implied that there could be an error of more than one mile. This is not evident from sets giving a position as latitude and longitude.

Loran-C

Loran-C has chains covering the North Atlantic, Mediterranean, Norwegian Sea, East Coast of America, North and Central Pacific, and South-East Asia with probable extensions to the North Sea and South-East Atlantic. As it utilises skywave transmission as well as groundwave transmission it has a much greater range (1,000M) than Decca. At long ranges the accuracy is 200m, but this improves to 70m at closer distances.

Satellite navigation

For world-wide position fixing, the use of radio broadcasts from orbiting navigation satellites is by far the most effective. An early system with 5 satellites (TRANSIT) is being replaced by a system with 18 satellites (Global Positioning System or GPS) which overcomes the problem of long delays between fixes. The accuracy is potentially extremely high (16m) but for security reasons commercially available sets will have an accuracy of about 100m.

Transit
A network of five satellites circle the earth at a height of 600M and an orbital time of 107 minutes. Depending on the boat's position this gives a time between fixes of 35 to 100 minutes. The receiver measures the range difference between the boat and two positions of the satellite to get one position line, then repeats the process later for a second position line. The point of intersection of these two lines (and a third if available) gives the boat's position. The range difference is obtained by measuring the doppler shift of the satellite's transmitted frequency, due primarily to the satellite's own motion, but also taking into account the boat's motion. The accuracy of the system depends on the accuracy of the input course and speed.

Global Positioning System
A network of 18 satellites will orbit the earth at a height of 10,000M with their orbital plane at 55° to the equator. The satellites transmit continuously to earth on two frequencies in the D band (1 to 2 GHz) and supply users with their position, velocity and time. Time is obtained from three atomic clocks which are so accurate that they will gain or lose only one second in 50,000 years. The satellites have an elaborate control system. There are five ground control monitor stations located around the earth to receive technical telemetered data from the satellites. The master control station sifts all the information it receives and transmits to the satellites their own true positions in space and the satellites in turn transmit their positions to the ground users.

   A ship will have a two-channel receiver. To use the receiver, switch it on and enter DR position, course and speed, and ship's time. The receiver then searches for available satellites, selects the most suitable, and starts tracking them. From each such satellite it receives the satellite's position, its number and accurate time. The receiver then calculates the satellite's range by measuring the time of receipt of the signal and multiplying the time taken for the signal to come from the satellite by the speed of radio waves in air. The receiver has thus located itself on a sphere of radius R_1, whose centre is the transmitting satellite. The receiver then measures the range of the second and third satellites to define spheres of radius R_2 and R_3. The receiver can then work out the point where the spheres intersect and displays this point as latitude and longitude.

Communications

VHF Radio Telephone
Many small craft are fitted with a VHF (very high frequency) radio telephone. It is a radio transmitter/receiver (transceiver) that enables the skipper of such a craft to communicate with a coast radio station (connecting to the public exchange network), a port or harbour radio station, and other vessels. In particular he can communicate with the Coastguard and with marinas and yacht harbours; but, most important, he can summon assistance in distress or in an emergency. With the exception of the latter instance, any person who uses the radio for transmission must have an operator's licence or be directly supervised by a licence holder. This is because the operation of a radio telephone allows anyone to listen to any transmission: so there has to be a strict discipline controlling any transmissions. It is not difficult to learn and it is in the interest of all skippers to become qualified.

In emergency or distress it is important that *all* the crew should understand the procedures, see back of chart 15.

The Coastguard has a VHF radio direction finder and, in *emergencies*, will inform a boat of its position.

For long distance passage making some skippers carry emergency position indicating radio beacons (EPIRBs). When activated these transmit an alarm tone on aircraft distress frequencies which enable the distressed boat or liferaft to be located.

Chapter Sixteen

Coastal Passage: Outward Bound

We have obtained the use of a sailing boat which is lying on one of the Sailing Club moorings off Christchurch Quay. The boat's name is *Plover*. She has a length of 7.9m and a draught of 1.0m. She is sloop rigged and has an outboard engine. Her normal cruising speed under sail is 4k and under power it is 3k. On 10th July we expect to be able to get on board at 0900 and would like to sail down to Swanage to anchor, possibly staying overnight. The weather forecast is: wind south to south east force 2 to 3, weather hazy, visibility moderate.

Preparation

Study chart 15. Find Christchurch Quay and Swanage Bay noting the anchorage in the latter. With moderate visibility (5M or less) a passage along the coast would be preferred. The wind is good for sailing, though there will be a little swell at the entrance to Christchurch harbour. Extending from Hengistbury Head is Christchurch Ledge which may cause a disturbed sea but no danger in a Force 3 wind as long as Beerpan Rocks are left well clear. We will need some clearing bearings or clearing transits for this. Following the coastline westwards towards Bournemouth should present no problems; and there are some convenient yellow buoys to help with our navigation. From Bournemouth we can cross over towards the entrance to Poole harbour, continuing towards Swanage. The anchorage seems clear to the north west of the pier with plenty of landmarks in the town. The seabed is fine sand (fS) in the anchorage.

Tides. See Extract 3 p. 119 and Extract 4 p. 120.

Height of tide required to clear bar in the entrance channel (charted depth 0_1) will be $1.0+0.5-0.1=1.4$m (draught+safe clearance−charted depth). Fill in tidal curve diagram, Fig 7.6. Earliest time to

	LW Time	Height	HW Time	Height	LW Time	Height	Range
Portsmouth GMT	0317	1.0	1027	4.4	1543	1.0	3.4
Differences	−0035	−0.7		−2.6	−0035	−0.7	mid
Christchurch	0242	0.3		1.8	1508	0.3	range
Add 1 hour	0100				0100		
Christchurch BST	0342				1608		

cross the bar is LW+2h 50m or 0632. The latest time to cross the bar is LW−3h 00m or 1308: so we must clear Christchurch entrance by 1308. There are no tidal constraints at Swanage.

Tidal Streams. The tidal stream diagram on chart 15 refers to HW at Portsmouth and LW at Poole (Town Quay) and Portsmouth. (The time of LW at Poole Town Quay and Portsmouth are nearly the same.) See Extract 3 p. 119.

	LW	HW	LW	HW
Portsmouth GMT	0317	1027	1543	2247
Add 1 hour	+0100	+0100	+0100	+0100
Portsmouth BST	0417	1127	1643	2347

Average range: 3.4m which is 0.3 down from springs (Portsmouth: spring range=4.1m, neap range=2.0m).

The only relevant tidal diamond is B off Poole entrance. The south-going stream is from HW−1 to HW+4 or 1027 to 1527. The north-going stream is from HW+5 to HW−2 or 1627 to 2147.

The avoid the foul tide off Poole entrance, we should aim to be in Swanage Bay before 1627.

The distance from Christchurch entrance to Swanage is 13M. At a boat speed of 4k under sail the passage time will be 3h 15m, though the favourable tidal stream may reduce this period. We must be outside Christchurch entrance by 1308 and we would like to be at Swanage by 1627. If the wind is predominantly south-east force 3 (SE 3), there is no problem. If the wind dies away and the passage is made under power at 3k, the passage time should not exceed 4h 20m which will be just about acceptable.

Refer to any sailing directions (see the reverse of chart 15) and yachtsmen's almanacs (see Extract 6 p. 121) for details of any local navigational information that might be relevant to the passage.

Passage

Variation 5°W used

The following is an extract from the deck log of *Plover*:

FROM: *Christchurch*   **TO:** *Swanage*   **DATE:** *10th July*

TIME		LOG	COURSE (°M)	WIND	BARO
1100	Slipped from mooring at Christchurch Quay Under power. Set courses to follow buoyed channel out of Christchurch harbour			SE 2	1024
1215	Crossed bar. Hoisted mainsail and working jib				
1230	Off Christchurch entrance. Set course 207°M. Stopped engine. Set log to zero. Leeway negligible.	0.0	207	SE 3	
1240	Established clearing bearing of 004°M on yellow buoy off groynes to keep clear of Beerpan Rocks				
1245	N end of sandbar at Christchurch entrance 012°M CG Lookout on Hengistbury Head in transit with beacon on end of groyne bearing 307°M. Altered course to 283°M	1.0	283		
1300		2.1	283	SE 3	
1303	Yellow buoy abeam. Altered course 273°M	2.2	273		
1340	Water Tower 063°M Hotel in Bournemouth 284°M Boscombe Pierhead in transit with yellow buoy 335°M	4.6	273		
1400	Yellow buoy off Bournemouth Pier abeam. Altered course 209°M	6.0	209	SE 3	1025
1421	St Peter's Church Spire 017°M Haven Hotel 265°M	7.4	209		
1445	Poole Fairway buoy 209°M Training Bank beacon 270°M East Hook buoy 323°M	9.0	209		
1458	Poole Fairway buoy abeam to stbd. Altered course 201°M	9.9	201		
1500		10.0	201	SE 3	
1504	Poole Fairway buoy 021°M Old Harry rock 295°M Altered course 209°M	10.3	209		
1522	Left hand edge of Durlston Head 209°M Swanage Methodist Church Spire 243°M Altered course 243°M	11.5	243		
1531	Monument on seafront in transit with Church Spire 243°M Maintained course to keep on transit Started engine. Dropped sails				
1540	Swanage Pierhead in transit with left hand edge of Peveril Point Altered course 123°M	12.4	123		

1545   Anchored off Swanage Pier, Depth of water   12.5   ESE 3   1026
2.7m. 10m of anchor cable let out. Anchor
bearings: Pierhead in transit with Peveril
Point, end of Jetty 221°M

Having anchored at Swanage a nasty swell is beginning to build up. Also the wind is shifting towards the east and blowing straight into the anchorage. The barometer is rising rapidly which may mean that the wind strength could increase. It would be prudent to leave Swanage and go into Poole Harbour.

QUESTIONS

16.1   From the extract from *Plover*'s deck log, plot the passage on chart 15.

16.2   Plates 4 to 17 are a series of views that might have been taken during the passage. Study them in conjunction with chart 15 and try to work out the latitude and longitude of the position from which the photograph was taken. (*Note:* A 'chine' is a name used in Dorset and the Isle of Wight to define a deep narrow ravine which may appear as a marked cleft in a cliff face.)

16.3   Study Plate 18. Can you identify the central feature? At what bearing (approximately) from the central feature has the photograph been taken? If the boat, from which the photograph was taken, proceeds on a northerly course, what will happen to the central feature?

Chapter Seventeen

Coastal Passage: Inward Bound

It is 1600 on 10th July and the yacht *Plover* (described in Chapter 16) is at anchor in Swanage Bay. The wind has shifted to the east and the increasing swell is making the anchorage uncomfortable. It is decided to enter Poole harbour possibly going as far as Wareham.

Preparation

Study chart 15. From Swanage Bay there are no hazards northward to Poole Fairway buoy. From the Fairway buoy, the Swash Channel is well buoyed with green conical buoys to starboard and red can-shaped buoys to port. There is a chain ferry between North Haven Point and South Haven Point. Turning to starboard in front of Brownsea Castle there is a south cardinal buoy marking the division between two channels: we will take Middle Ship Channel branching to the left. On approaching Poole Town the Little Channel branches off to the right; but we will continue straight on leaving the Ro-Ro Terminal to starboard. The buoyed channel winds about a little between areas of moorings before dividing with a narrow channel to the right leading to Rockley Point. The Wareham Channel is to the left across an open expanse of water; but there is a line of red port hand buoys leading to a line of perches (thin posts). Beyond the perches is the River Frome leading to Wareham. The charted depth in several places is 0.1m (0_1). There appear to be several boatyards where there are mooring facilities for yachtsmen: Cobbs Quay Marina, Quay West Marina, Dorset Yacht Co, Rotork Boat Park, Ridge Wharf Yacht Centre and alongside the quays at Poole and Wareham.

Tides. See Chapter 16 and Tidal Information panel on chart 15. HW Portsmouth is at 2347 (BST). The range of the tide at Portsmouth is 3.4m which is about one third (0.3) down from springs. HW at Poole

104

(Entrance) is 3h 30m before HW Portsmouth (interpolating between −2h 40m at springs and −5h 10m at neaps) which is 2017. HW at Poole (Town Quay) is 3h 00m before HW Portsmouth or 2047 at which time the height of tide will be about 2.0m above chart datum. This means that there will be a rising tide until about 2030 all the way up to Wareham and, generally, sufficient height of tide for *Plover* to clear the areas with a charted depth of 0.1m.

Tidal Streams. See Chapter 16 and chart 15. The relevant tidal diamonds are B off Poole Fairway buoy and C to H throughout the length of Poole harbour. LW at Portsmouth is at 1643 (BST). At tidal diamond F the flood tide is between LW+30m (1713) and LW+5 (2143). At tidal diamond C the flood tide is from LW (1643) to LW+4 (2043). At tidal diamond B the north-going stream is from HW+5 (1627) to HW−2 (2147).

The distance from Swanage to Wareham is 15M. It would be reasonable to sail from Swanage until a point half way up the Swash Channel (a distance of 5M) but then it might be prudent to proceed to Wareham under power or under reduced sail (foresail only). So the time taken to reach Wareham will be: (5M at 4k plus 10M at 3k)=4h 35m. Leaving straight away (at 1600) would mean an ETA at Wareham of 2035. As this does not include any allowance for favourable tidal stream and is well within the hours of daylight, then the timing for the passage is quite acceptable.

QUESTIONS

17.1 Using the extract from the deck log of the yacht *Plover* as shown in Chapter 16 as an example, write up a simulated deck log for the passage from Swanage to Wareham assuming a departure time of 1630, a boat speed of 4k to the chain ferry between N Haven Pt and S Haven Pt and 3k thereafter.

17.2 Using Plates 19 to 26 identify the views and work out the position from which each photograph was taken.

17.3 Plate 27 shows a view taken on the way to an alternative destination had it been decided not to proceed as far as Wareham. Identify the view.

Chapter Eighteen

Test Paper

Chart 15

Use variation $5°W$. Times are BST and answers should be given in BST.

A1. On 5th August a boat is sailing from Yarmouth (Isle of Wight) to the anchorage in Studland Bay. The wind is west force 4. At 1010, log 10.7, she passes the Fairway buoy off the Needles. She is on the starboard tack making good a course of 230°M with leeway estimated at 5°. At 1100, log 13.8, she tacks through 90°. At 1110, log 14.5, the following bearings are taken:

Anvil Point lighthouse   275°M

Water tower to the left of Hengistbury Head   350°M

Plot the position at 1110.

A2. Assuming a boat speed of 4k, at what time should the boat tack in order to arrive at the Poole Fairway buoy on the next tack? What will be her ETA at the buoy? Leeway is 5°. Use tidal diamond D until 1300 then tidal diamond C.

A3. At 1210, log 18.6, course 320°M, bearings are taken as follows:

Anvil Point lighthouse	247°M
Right hand edge of Handfast Point	281°M
Water tower	015°M

Plot the position at 1210.

A4. At 1215 the wind starts dying away. At 1300 it is decided to motor to Studland Bay. At 1310, log 19.9, the following bearings are taken:

Left hand edge of Durlston Head	233°M
Left hand edge of Haven Hotel	305°M

Plot the position at 1310.

A5. From the 1310 position, what is the magnetic course to steer to

Poole Fairway buoy. Use tidal diamond C and a boat speed of 3k. What is the ETA at the buoy?

A6.   Steering the course from Question A5, at 1355, log 22.1, Poole Fairway buoy bears 198°M at a distance of 0.3M. What has been the direction and rate of the tidal stream between 1310 and 1355?

A7.   At 1355 the boat steers towards Poole Fairway buoy which is reached at 1405. She then alters course for the anchorage in Studland Bay. The estimated tidal stream is 290°T 0.3k. At a boat speed of 3k, what is the magnetic course to steer to the anchorage? What is the ETA? How can the boat's ground track be checked?

A8.   The boat anchors at 1420. On arrival the depth of water is measured as 4.0m. If remaining overnight, what will be the least depth of water in the anchorage and how much anchor cable should be let out? What is the quality of the bottom? Use tidal differences for Swanage and the tidal curve diagram for Christchurch.

Answers to Questions

1.1 Chart 15 is a **much larger scale** chart than chart 12 so will include more detail.

1.2 Poole Harbour and approaches.

1.3a. The latitude scale.
  b. The longitude scale.

1.4 By using the latitude and longitude scales as a reference.

1.5 One nautical mile per hour.

2.1 During projection distortion occurs on the chart. On a mercator projection chart the distance scale increases as latitude increases, therefore **one minute of latitude is equivalent to one nautical mile** *only* **in the area of the boat's position.**

2.2 Meridians of longitude appear as **straight lines** in a north–south direction. **Parallels of latitude** appear as **straight parallel lines** in an east–west direction (at right angles to meridians of longitude). Any **Rhumb Line course crosses all meridians and parallels of latitude at the same angle.**

2.3 There is **too much distortion.**

2.4 The **Greenwich meridian** which passes through London.

2.5 50° 38'.5.

3.1 Anvil Point lighthouse.

3.2a. 0.1M.
  b. 0.05M.

3.3a. 023°T.
   b. 4.7M.
   c. 1h 03m.

3.4   This should be close to East Hook buoy.

3.5   50° 36'.0N 1° 55'.0W.

CHAPTER FOUR

4.1   4° 58'W.

4.2a. 224°M, 143°M, 009°M.
   b. 352°T, 185°T, 012°T.

4.3a. 001°C, 004°C, 158°C.
   b. 231°M, 066°M, 289°M.

4.4   The deviation for *all three* bearings is 4°E which is the figure shown on the deviation table corresponding to the boat's heading of 060°C.
   a. Tower 089°T; Church 165°T; Monument 328°T.
   b. 2°W.

4.5   Well away from anything likely to cause deviation (electrical equipment, magnets, ferrous metal); accurately aligned with the fore-and-aft line of the boat; where it can easily be seen by the helmsman; and where it will not suffer damage.

CHAPTER FIVE

5.1   Symbols and Abbreviations used on Admiralty Charts (chart booklet 5011).

5.2a Wreck considered dangerous to surface navigation; Visitor's mooring; Marina.
   b. No. 17 green buoy; Anchorage; Radiobeacon.
   c. Fine sand.

5.3   Just under 2m.

5.4   Tide race on the ebb.

5.5   45m.

CHAPTER SIX

6.1   The lowest level to which the tide is expected to fall due to astronomical conditions.

6.2   Yes: due to abnormal meteorological conditions such as high barometric pressure or strong offshore winds blowing for a period of several days.

6.3a. The depth of water below **Chart Datum.**

    b. In **metres and decimetres.**

6.4   **Mean High Water Springs (MHWS)** which is the mean of the spring tide high waters throughout the year.

6.5 At **spring tides.**

CHAPTER SEVEN

7.1 From **Admiralty Tide Tables, Yachtsmen's Almanacs** and local tide tables.

7.2 **3.8m.**

7.3 **4.2m.**

		HW		LW	Range
Dover	GMT	1517	6.1	1.1	5.0 (0.3 from Sps)
		+0100			
	BST	1617			

Interval: HW+3h 03m

7.4 **1228 BST.**

		HW		LW	Range
Dover	GMT	1348	5.9	1.5	4.4 (0.5 from Sps)
Differences		+0020	−1.6	−0.6	
Ramsgate	GMT	1408	4.3	0.9	
		+0100			
	BST	1508			

Interval: HW−2h 40m

7.5 **1.3m.**

		HW	LW		Range
Portsmouth	GMT	4.0	0738	1.3	1.7 (Nps)
Differences		−1.4	−0025	−0.2	
Yarmouth	GMT	2.6	0713	1.1	
			+0100		
	BST		0813		

Interval: LW+2h 02m

CHAPTER EIGHT

8.1 **180°T 1.1 knots.**

8.2 **HW+6 to HW−1.** Six hours after high water to one hour before high water.

8.3 Tabulated values are mean values. **Considerable variation may occur at spring tides.**

8.4 Often the tidal streams in bays are slacker or on some occasions there is a contrary stream. In this case the boats are **lying head to wind indicating that there is little or no tidal stream.**

8.5 **Sail close to the buoy and look at the tidal stream around it.**

CHAPTER NINE

9.1a. i. **A white tower.** ii. **A white light flashing every 10 seconds.**

  b. **17M.** In the light characteristics the figure 24M is the nominal range of the light (the range at which the light would be visible when the meteorological visibility is 10 miles). This does not take into account the curvature of the earth. There are tables in Yachtsmen's Almanacs which give the range of a light knowing the height of the light and the height of the observer's eye. For the height of the light, allowance also has to be made for the state of the tide. For a height of eye of 2m and a height of light of 45m, the range of a light would be 17M.

  c. **A horn sounding 3 blasts every 30 seconds.**

9.2 No: it is obscured. **The castle on Durlston Head, Handfast Point.**

9.3 **There is no major reason not to use the inshore passage at night as it is adequately lit.** Check that the characteristics of the white light are those of Poole Fairway buoy, then plot the position on the chart. Proceed on a northerly course until reaching the white sector of the occulting light, but keep a good lookout for the unlit East Hook buoy. Alter course to 311°M to stay in the white sector until the East Looe buoy (quick flashing red) is passed to port. Alter course to 255°T (260°M) heading for the main channel watching out for the unlit north cardinal beacon which is left to port. Keep a careful check on the depth using the echo-sounder. The depth will also indicate when the main channel has been reached.

9.4 **The ferry is about to start.** Officially **sound 4 blasts on the fog horn** (or **klaxon**) to warn the ferry allowing it time to manoeuvre. In practice it would be courteous to give way to the ferry.

9.5 a. Maintain a course to keep Anvil Point light visible clear of Durlston Head. When the main lights in the town of Swanage can be seen clear of Peveril Point, identify the 2 fixed red vertical lights on Swanage pier and use them as a clearing bearing (which should not be greater than 277°M) to proceed towards the anchorage off Swanage.

  b. **Two fixed red vertical lights.**

CHAPTER TEN

10.1 Course 015°T, Water track 015°T, Distance run 1.9M
   a. **50° 37′.3N 1° 53′.7W**
   b. **50° 37′.6N 1° 53′.2W**
   c. **021°T**
   d. **4.4k**

10.2 Course 350°T, Water track 350°T, Distance run 2.5M
     Course 090°T, Water track 090°T, Distance run 2.5M
     EP 50° 39′.7N 1° 44′.0W

10.3 Course 001°T, Distance run 1.7M
     344°T 1.4k

10.4 Course 051°M, 046°T, Water track 056°T
     Course 320°M, 315°T, Water track 305°T
     Tidal streams: (A) 049° 1.0k (B) 354° 0.5k
     EP (1250) 50° 38′.4N 1° 49′.1W
     EP (1320) 50° 39′.8N 1° 51′.7W

10.5 Course (1600–1700) 283°M, 278°T, Water track 273°T, Distance run 4.1M
     Course (1700–1703) 231°M, 226°T, Water track 226°T, Distance run 0.2M
     Course (1703–1749) 231°M, 226°T, Water track 226°T, Distance run 2.7M
     EP (1700) 50° 42′.6N 1° 52′.0W
     EP (1749) 50° 40′.7N 1° 55′.3W
     East Hook buoy

CHAPTER ELEVEN

11.1a. **50° 35′.4N 1° 57′.5W.**
   b. **A sounding would have shown that the boat was over the 10m depth contour.** With only 2 bearings the angle of cut should be around 90°: the right hand edge of Durlston Head would have given a better cut.
   c. The most probable cause is a **tidal stream stronger than anticipated.**

11.2a. The true bearing of the transit of the beacons (from the chart) is 354°T, hence the magnetic bearing is 359°M. The deviation is therefore **4°E.**
   b. **No:** it is only valid for the boat's present heading of 263°C and will alter as the heading changes.
   c. **No:** transit bears 354°T.
   d. The hand-bearing compass is only free from deviation if it is

used **well clear of all magnetic influences.**

11.3 Anvil Point light 279°T. Course 010°T.
Water track 015°T.
Handfast Point 348°T. Distance run 1.9M.
Tidal stream 049°T 1.0k.

a. 50° 37'.5N 1° 54'.9W.
b. The accuracy of a transferred position line (running fix) depends on the **correct assessment of the tidal stream and leeway** together with an **accurate course and distance run** from the log.
c. **168°T Handfast Point 1.1M.**

11.4 Bournemouth pier   281°T
Boscombe pier   047°T
Hotel   000°T
Yellow buoy   262°T

a. 50° 42'.6N 1° 51'.2W.
b. The three bearings of the shore landmarks intersect at the same point: the **buoy is not exactly in the position shown on the chart.**

11.5a. **No:** the depth corrected to charted depth is 10.5m which only indicates that the boat is in the vicinity of the 10m depth contour. Approximate position 50° 42'.9N 1° 46'.0W.
b. The boat is heading for Beerpan Rocks (at a distance of 0.6M) with insufficient depth of water to clear them. She would **alter course to 114°M** until the CG Lookout and the beacon on the end of the groyne are in transit.

CHAPTER TWELVE

12.1 Water track 070°T. Course 080°T, **085°M**. Speed made good 4.1k.

12.2 Distance to go about 5M. Tidal stream 156°T 0.6k. Water track 221°T. Course 226°T, **231°M**. Speed made good 4.3k. Time taken 1h 08m. ETA **1858.**

12.3 Distance to go 3.9M. Tidal streams: (A) HW−3: 053°T 1.0k; (B) HW−2: 029°T 0.2k. Water track 288°T. Course 278°T, **283°M**. Distance made good 4.6M, speed made good 2.3k. Time taken 1h 42m. ETA **1732.**

12.4 Tidal stream: 1150-1250, HW−5: 049°T 1.0k; 1250-1350, HW−4: 354°T 0.5k. Speed made good 4.0k. (It is not necessary to plot a tidal vector for the first part as the tidal stream is along track: speed made good=speed+tidal stream=3.0+1.0=4.0). Time taken 1h. Water track 050°T. Course 040°T, **045°M**. The boat tacks in position 50° 38′.0N 1° 50′.8W. Distance to go to buoy 2.7M. Time taken 51m. Water track 282°T. Course 292°T, **297°M**. Speed made good 3.2k. ETA **1341**.

12.5   Distance to go about 3.4M. Tidal stream 344°T 1.4k. (Plot 30 minute vector: 344°T 0.7M.) Water track 023°T. Course 023°T, **028°M**. Distance made good 3.6M; speed made good 7.2k. Time taken 29 minutes. ETA **0929**.

CHAPTER THIRTEEN

13.1   a. Local weather centre.
       b. By listening to the shipping forecast.

13.2   **Listen to the Coast Radio station** at Niton at 0833 (GMT) or contact the **Coastguard** (Channel 16 then Channel 67) and request a weather report.

13.3   The prolonged blast indicates a power-driven vessel underway. The immediate action is to **slow down and keep well over to the starboard side of the channel** sounding the appropriate fog signal. The subsequent action may be to **alter course for Studland Bay and anchor until the visibility improves.**

13.4   As the wind has been blowing in the same direction for two days, a wave pattern will have been built up and may not disappear immediately with the wind shift. The new wind direction may cause a new wave pattern superimposed on the other. The coastline down to Anvil Point will give some protection but there are tide races on the ebb tide around the headlands which cause steep seas that will be unpleasant if not dangerous.
   a. **The motor boat would roll and pitch heavily in the seas with spray on deck. She would need to slow down in the rough seas off the headlands.**
   b. **The fin-keeled sailing boat would be heeled well over even if reefed with plenty of spray on deck and pitching heavily. Progress will be slow.**
   c. **The bilge-keel sailing boat will make little or no progress in the heavy seas. She would pitch and roll uncomfortably and the waves may frequently break over the deck.**

13.5a. **Less than 2M.**
    b. **Between 35k and 45k.**
    c. **Beaufort Force 7: 28k–33k.**
    d. **Beaufort Force 4: 11k–16k.**
    e. **From 12 to 24 hours hence.**

CHAPTER SIXTEEN

16.1 *Refer to plot (see front endpaper).*

16.2 Plate 4 **Christchurch harbour entrance** (50° 43'.4N 1° 43'.9W)

Plate 5 **Groyne off Hengistbury Head** (50° 42'.5N 1° 45'.0W)

Plate 6 **CG Lookout – Hengistbury Head** (50° 42'.6N 1° 45'.5W)

Plate 7 **Christchurch Priory** (50° 42'.6N 1° 46'.1W)

Plate 8 **Water Tower (conspic)** (50° 42'.6N 1° 48'.1W)

Plate 9 **Bournemouth – St Peter's church** (50° 42'.5N 1° 52'.3W)

Plate 10 **Bournemouth – Hotel (conspic)** (50° 42'.2N 1° 53'.4W)

Plate 11 **Poole Fairway – Handfast Point** (50° 39'.1N 1° 54'.7W)

Plate 12 **Handfast Point – Durlston Head** (50° 38'.8N 1° 55'.2W)

Plate 13 **Handfast Point** (50° 38'.5N 1° 55'.0W)

Plate 14 **Peveril Ledge – Durlston Head** (50° 36'.5N 1° 55'.9W)

Plate 15 **Peveril Point** (50° 36'.5N 1° 56'.5W)

Plate 16 **Swanage pier** (50° 36'.5N 1° 56'.7W)

Plate 17 **Swanage town** (50° 36'.6N 1° 57'.1W)

16.3 **Anvil Point lighthouse.** The photograph was taken on a bearing of 080°T from the lighthouse. The **lighthouse becomes obscured** from a more northerly position.

CHAPTER SEVENTEEN

17.1 The deck log might be entered as follows:

FROM: *Swanage*   TO: *Wareham*   DATE: *10th July*

TIME		LOG	COURSE (°M)	WIND	BARO
1630	*Weighed anchor in Swanage Bay. Set course 044°M under power*	*12.5*	*044*	*E4*	*1026*
1640	*Hoisted main and working jib. Stopped engine*	*13.1*	*044*		
1651	*Ballard Point abeam*	*13.8*	*044*		
1700		*14.4*	*044*	*E4*	*1026*
1703	*Handfast Point abeam. Altered course 344°M for Swash channel*	*14.5*	*344*		
1708	*Poole Fairway buoy abeam*	*14.9*	*344*		

TIME		LOG	COURSE (°M)	WIND	BARO
1714	Entered Swash channel between Bar buoy and No 2 buoy. Followed channel	15.3	344		
1733	No 16 buoy to port. Started engine and lowered sails	16.5	Var		
1735	Passed chain ferry				
1744	Passed Bell buoy opposite Brownsea Castle. Followed Middle Ship channel	17.2	Var		
1750	Shipping forecast: Portland, Wight SE 5–6 Moderate to good				
1800		18.1	Var	ESE3	1027
1807	Stakes buoy abeam. Followed Wareham channel	18.5	Var		
1831	Passed Dorset Yacht Co jetty	19.9	Var		
1900	Gigger's Isle to port	21.6	Var	SE2	1027
1926	Passed Ridge Wharf yacht centre	23.1	Var		
1950	Secured to visitor's berth on Wareham Quay. Engine stopped	24.5	Var		

17.2   Plate 19 **Ballard Point** (50°37'.5N 1°55'.8W)
Plate 20 **Haven Hotel** (50°40'.8N 1°56'.8W)
Plate 21 **East Looe channel** (50°41'.0N 1°56'.1W)
Plate 22 **Chain ferry** (50°40'.8N 1°56'.8W)
Plate 23 **Bell buoy** (50°41'.3N 1°56'.8W)
Plate 24 **Ro-Ro terminal** (50° 42'.4N 1° 59'.0W)
Plate 25 **No. 67 buoy** (50°42'.2N 1°59'.6W)
Plate 26 **No. 76 buoy** (50°42'.7N 2°02'.1W)

17.3   Plate 27 **Poole bridge** (50°42'.7N 1°59'.3W)

TEST PAPER

Refer to plot for answers A1 to A8 (see back endpaper).

A1.   50° 35'.5N 1° 44'.6W.

Mag Course	Var	True Course	Leeway	Water Track	
230	5°W	225	5°	220	stbd tack
320	5°W	315	5°	320	port tack

A2.   Plot the ground track on the port tack for a period of 2 hours using tidal diamond D. To reach Poole Fairway buoy it will be necessary to tack at around 1300. From the buoy plot the ground track on the starboard tack, using tidal diamond C, for a period of, say, 30 minutes from 1300. Extend this ground track backwards to intersect with that of the port tack. Work out from the distance and speed made good on the port tack the ETA at the point of intersection. This is **1255.**

Similarly using the distance and speed made good on the starboard tack, the ETA at Poole Fairway buoy is **1329**.

HW Portsmouth is at 0740 BST and it is neap tides.

A3. 50° 38'.2N 1° 49'.4W

A4. 50° 38'.9N 1° 51'.1W

A5. Course to steer 265°M. ETA 1354.

A6. Tidal Stream 353°T 0.9k.
From the 1310 position plot the water track to obtain the DR position for 1355. The direction and distance of the 1355 fix from the 1355 DR position is the tidal stream experienced. Note that the 1355 fix used the bearing of the buoy *from* the yacht. The actual tidal stream on a passage is usually slightly different from that predicted from tidal diamonds which are calculated for the exact position of the diamond.

A7. Course to steer 248°M. ETA 1418. Measure the bearing of Poole Fairway buoy from the anchorage (073°M) and approach the anchorage maintaining a course to keep the buoy steady on that bearing. If an object or a transit can be identified ahead on the shoreline, then use that instead.

A8. Least depth of water (at next LW) **3.7m**. Length of anchor cable: **13m** if all chain, or **21m** if a combination of chain and nylon warp. The bottom is **fine sand** (fS).

	Time	LW Height	HW Height	LW Height	Range
Portsmouth	1210 GMT	1.8	4.0	1.6	2.2
Differences	−0105	−0.5	−2.4	−0.5	neaps
Swanage	1105 GMT	1.3	1.6	1.1	
Add 1 hour	+0100				
Swanage	1205 BST				

1420 is LW+2h 15m: height of tide is 1.4m
Charted depth=4.0−1.4=2.6m
Depth of water at *next* LW=1.1+2.6=3.7m
Depth of water at next HW=1.6+2.6=4.2m
Length of chain=3× max. depth=3×4.2=12.6 or 13m
Length of chain plus warp=5× max. depth=5×4.2=21.0 or 21m

Extract 1

Lat. 51°07′N. Long. 1°19′E.

DOVER
HIGH & LOW WATER

MAY

Time	m		Time	m
1 0036 / 0757 / F 1300 / 2006	6.4 / 0.9 / 6.2 / 1.1	**16**	0017 / 0745 / Sa 1248 / 2008	6.4 / 0.8 / 6.4 / 0.9
2 0107 / 0827 / Sa 1331 / 2042	6.2 / 1.1 / 6.0 / 1.3	**17**	0109 / 0833 / Su 1341 / 2057	6.3 / 0.9 / 6.2 / 1.0
3 0137 / 0901 / Su 1405 / 2118	5.9 / 1.4 / 5.8 / 1.6	**18**	0206 / 0925 / M 1434 / 2152	6.0 / 1.2 / 6.0 / 1.2
4 0212 / 0938 / M 1447 / 2159	5.5 / 1.7 / 5.5 / 1.9	**19**	0307 / 1026 / Tu 1531 / 2257	5.8 / 1.5 / 5.8 / 1.4
5 0301 / 1020 / Tu 1545 / 2249	5.2 / 2.1 / 5.2 / 2.1	**20**	0414 / 1136 / W 1637	5.6 / 1.6 / 5.6
6 0419 / 1115 / W 1701 / 2354	4.9 / 2.3 / 5.1 / 2.2	**21**	0010 / 0539 / Th 1250 / 1800	1.5 / 5.5 / 1.6 / 5.5
7 0550 / 1227 / Th 1817	4.8 / 2.4 / 5.1	**22**	0127 / 0659 / F 1404 / 1914	1.4 / 5.6 / 1.5 / 5.7

JUNE

Time	m		Time	m
1 0120 / 0840 / M 1348 / 2101	5.8 / 1.4 / 5.9 / 1.5	**16**	0208 / 0934 / Tu 1426 / 2159	6.2 / 1.0 / 6.3 / 0.9
2 0157 / 0915 / Tu 1427 / 2141	5.6 / 1.6 / 5.8 / 1.7	**17**	0300 / 1028 / W 1517 / 2254	6.1 / 1.2 / 6.1 / 1.1
3 0242 / 0955 / W 1515 / 2224	5.4 / 1.8 / 5.6 / 1.8	**18**	0356 / 1123 / Th 1612 / 2353	5.9 / 1.4 / 5.9 / 1.2
4 0342 / 1041 / Th 1614 / 2318	5.2 / 2.0 / 5.5 / 1.9	**19**	0459 / 1221 / F 1716	5.7 / 1.5 / 5.8
5 0452 / 1136 / F 1719	5.1 / 2.1 / 5.4	**20**	0055 / 0608 / Sa 1323 / 1824	1.4 / 5.6 / 1.7 / 5.8
6 0021 / 0557 / Sa 1243 / 1819	1.9 / 5.2 / 2.1 / 5.5	**21**	0201 / 0712 / Su 1426 / 1928	1.5 / 5.6 / 1.7 / 5.8
7 0127 / 0653 / Su 1349 / 1914	1.8 / 5.6 / 2.0 / 5.7	**22**	0305 / 0809 / M 1525 / 2026	1.5 / 5.7 / 1.7 / 5.9

JULY

Time	m		Time	m
1 0138 / 0857 / W 1405 / 2121	5.9 / 1.5 / 6.1 / 1.4	**16**	0237 / 1013 / Th 1450 / 2235	6.3 / 1.0 / 6.4 / 0.9
2 0219 / 0929 / Th 1444 / 2159	5.7 / 1.6 / 6.0 / 1.5	**17**	0324 / 1052 / F 1539 / 2319	6.1 / 1.3 / 6.2 / 1.2
3 0305 / 1006 / F 1531 / 2240	5.6 / 1.8 / 5.8 / 1.7	**18**	0416 / 1134 / Sa 1633	5.9 / 1.6 / 6.0
4 0400 / 1049 / Sa 1624 / 2329	5.5 / 1.9 / 5.7 / 1.9	**19**	0008 / 0516 / Su 1224 / 1737	1.5 / 5.6 / 1.9 / 5.7
5 0458 / 1143 / Su 1720	5.4 / 2.1 / 5.7	**20**	0107 / 0627 / M 1328 / 1850	1.8 / 5.4 / 2.1 / 5.6
6 0028 / 0557 / M 1248 / 1819	1.8 / 5.4 / 2.1 / 5.7	**21**	0219 / 0737 / Tu 1443 / 2001	2.0 / 5.4 / 2.1 / 5.6
7 0133 / 0657 / Tu 1359 / 1920	1.8 / 5.5 / 2.1 / 5.7	**22**	0327 / 0839 / W 1546 / 2101	2.0 / 5.6 / 2.0 / 5.6

AUGUST

Time	m		Time	m
1 0223 / 0934 / Sa 1442 / 2202	5.9 / 1.6 / 6.1 / 1.5	**16**	0335 / 1040 / Su 1552 / 2313	5.9 / 1.7 / 6.0 / 1.7
2 0304 / 1010 / Su 1524 / 2244	5.7 / 1.8 / 5.9 / 1.7	**17**	0431 / 1122 / M 1654	5.5 / 2.1 / 5.6
3 0356 / 1055 / M 1620 / 2337	5.5 / 2.0 / 5.7 / 1.9	**18**	0005 / 0546 / Tu 1225 / 1819	2.2 / 5.2 / 2.4 / 5.2
4 0459 / 1158 / Tu 1727	5.4 / 2.2 / 5.5	**19**	0126 / 0710 / W 1359 / 1944	2.4 / 5.2 / 2.5 / 5.2
5 0046 / 0612 / W 1319 / 1845	2.0 / 5.3 / 2.2 / 5.4	**20**	0254 / 0820 / Th 1524 / 2051	2.4 / 5.3 / 2.2 / 5.4
6 0206 / 0740 / Th 1449 / 2009	2.0 / 5.4 / 2.0 / 5.6	**21**	0357 / 0917 / F 1620 / 2145	2.1 / 5.6 / 1.9 / 5.6
7 0332 / 0903 / F 1614 / 2124	1.7 / 5.7 / 1.6 / 5.8	**22**	0447 / 1000 / Sa 1705 / 2224	1.6 / 5.9 / 1.6 / 5.8

WHEN TO ENTER — The best time is between −0200 and +0100 (Dover).
WHEN TO LEAVE — All times suitable, but caution required when meeting stream off ent.
RATE AND SET — The stream in the entrance and harbour vary considerably. E. going stream begins −0210 (Dover). Sets 068°, 4 knots (Springs), 2½ knots (Neaps). W. going stream begins +0430 (Dover). Sets 224°. 2½ knots (Springs), 1½ knots (Neaps).

Extract 2

TIDAL DIFFERENCES ON DOVER

PLACE	MHW Tm. Diff. h. min.	MHW Ht. Diff. m.	MLW Tm. Diff. h. min.	MLW Ht. Diff. m.	HWS m.	HWN m.	CD m.	POSITION
Hastings	−0 05	+0.6	−0 30	0.0	9.0	7.3	1.5	Entrance
Rye (Apprs.)	0 00	+0.8	—	—	6.2	4.5	−1.5	Bar near entrance
Dungeness	−0 15	+1.2	−0 15	+0.2	15.3	13.6	7.3	West Road Anche.
Folkestone	−0 10	+0.4	−0 10	0.0	5.5	3.1	−1.6	Alongside Sth Quay
Dover	0 00	0.0	0 00	0.0	7.1	5.7	0.4	Entce. Granville Dock
Deal	+0 15	−0.4	+0 05	0.0	10.1	9.0	4.0	Pier Head
Richborough	+0 15	−1.0	—	—	2.8	1.7	−0.9	Chan to
Ramsgate	+0 20	−1.6	−0 07	−0.6	5.0	3.9	0.1	Entrance

NOTE: Rye should be carefully considered. It dries out, tidal streams are strong and rough weather can make Rye Bay very dangerous for small vessels.
Folkestone is unsuitable except in emergency.
Ramsgate is an excellent harbour for all small yachts.

Extract 3

PORTSMOUTH

HIGH & LOW WATER   **GMT** ADD 1 HOUR MARCH 29 – OCTOBER 25 FOR B.S.T.

MAY

Day	TIME	M		TIME	M	Day
1 F	0059 / 0610 / 1327 / 1827	4.5 / 0.8 / 4.4 / 1.1	**16** SA	0047 / 0606 / 1320 / 1829	4.7 / 0.6 / 4.5 / 0.9	
2 SA	0131 / 0642 / 1403 / 1858	4.4 / 0.9 / 4.2 / 1.3	**17** SU	0132 / 0653 / 1413 / 1917	4.5 / 0.7 / 4.4 / 1.1	
3 SU	0203 / 0717 / 1441 / 1937	4.2 / 1.2 / 4.1 / 1.6	**18** M	0222 / 0744 / 1510 / 2012	4.3 / 0.9 / 4.3 / 1.4	
4 M	0240 / 0800 / 1524 / 2026	4.0 / 1.5 / 3.9 / 1.9	**19** TU	0319 / 0843 / 1616 / 2119	4.1 / 1.1 / 4.2 / 1.6	
5 TU	0327 / 0852 / 1620 / 2132	3.7 / 1.7 / 3.7 / 2.1	**20** W	0425 / 0953 / 1729 / 2237	3.9 / 1.3 / 4.1 / 1.7	
6 W	0430 / 1000 / 1732 / 2254	3.5 / 1.9 / 3.6 / 2.1	**21** TH	0544 / 1112 / 1845 / 2357	3.8 / 1.4 / 4.1 / 1.6	
7 TH	0549 / 1122 / 1848	3.4 / 1.9 / 3.6	**22** F	0702 / 1226 / 1951	3.8 / 1.3 / 4.2	
8 F	0013 / 0707 / 1234 / 1952	1.9 / 3.5 / 1.7 / 3.8	**23** SA	0104 / 0807 / 1327 / 2043	1.4 / 4.0 / 1.2 / 4.3	
9 SA	0113 / 0808 / 1329 / 2039	1.7 / 3.7 / 1.4 / 4.1	**24** SU	0158 / 0859 / 1417 / 2127	1.2 / 4.1 / 1.1 / 4.4	
10 SU	0158 / 0855 / 1413 / 2121	1.4 / 4.0 / 1.1 / 4.3	**25** M	0242 / 0944 / 1500 / 2207	1.1 / 4.3 / 1.0 / 4.5	
11 M	0238 / 0935 / 1454 / 2201	1.4 / 4.3 / 0.9 / 4.6	**26** TU	0322 / 1026 / 1542 / 2245	1.0 / 4.4 / 1.0 / 4.6	

JUNE

Day	TIME	M		TIME	M	Day
1 M	0143 / 0659 / 1423 / 1919	4.1 / 1.2 / 4.1 / 1.6	**16** TU	0213 / 0739 / 1503 / 2007	4.4 / 0.8 / 4.5 / 1.3	
2 TU	0220 / 0738 / 1504 / 2004	4.0 / 1.3 / 4.0 / 1.7	**17** W	0307 / 0834 / 1602 / 2105	4.3 / 1.0 / 4.5 / 1.4	
3 W	0302 / 0822 / 1550 / 2055	3.8 / 1.5 / 3.9 / 1.8	**18** TH	0407 / 0934 / 1703 / 2209	4.1 / 1.1 / 4.4 / 1.5	
4 TH	0352 / 0916 / 1642 / 2155	3.7 / 1.6 / 3.9 / 1.9	**19** F	0512 / 1039 / 1807 / 2318	4.0 / 1.3 / 4.2 / 1.6	
5 F	0451 / 1017 / 1741 / 2301	3.6 / 1.6 / 3.8 / 1.8	**20** SA	0623 / 1147 / 1909	3.9 / 1.4 / 4.2	
6 SA	0557 / 1123 / 1843	3.6 / 1.6 / 3.9	**21** SU	0025 / 0732 / 1252 / 2006	1.5 / 3.9 / 1.4 / 4.2	
7 SU	0005 / 0702 / 1227 / 1939	1.7 / 3.8 / 1.5 / 4.1	**22** M	0125 / 0832 / 1349 / 2055	1.4 / 4.0 / 1.4 / 4.2	
8 M	0101 / 0800 / 1323 / 2031	1.5 / 4.0 / 1.3 / 4.3	**23** TU	0217 / 0924 / 1437 / 2141	1.3 / 4.1 / 1.4 / 4.3	
9 TU	0153 / 0854 / 1416 / 2122	1.3 / 4.2 / 1.1 / 4.5	**24** W	0303 / 1011 / 1523 / 2223	1.2 / 4.2 / 1.3 / 4.3	
10 W	0241 / 0946 / 1506 / 2211	1.0 / 4.4 / 1.0 / 4.6	**25** TH	0345 / 1055 / 1604 / 2303	1.1 / 4.3 / 1.3 / 4.4	
11 TH	0330 / 1038 / 1556 / O 2300	0.9 / 4.5 / 0.9 / 4.7	**26** F	0425 / 1136 / 1643 / ● 2341	1.1 / 4.3 / 1.2 / 4.3	

JULY

Day	TIME	M		TIME	M	Day
1 W	0203 / 0719 / 1442 / 1941	4.0 / 1.1 / 4.2 / 1.5	**16** TH	0248 / 0815 / 1535 / 2041	4.5 / 0.8 / 4.7 / 1.3	
2 TH	0240 / 0756 / 1520 / 2021	4.0 / 1.2 / 4.2 / 1.5	**17** F	0338 / 0905 / 1626 / 2133	4.4 / 1.0 / 4.5 / 1.4	
3 F	0320 / 0837 / 1600 / 2106	3.9 / 1.3 / 4.1 / 1.6	**18** SA	0434 / 1000 / 1721 / 2233	4.1 / 1.3 / 4.3 / 1.6	
4 SA	0404 / 0925 / 1647 / 2159	3.9 / 1.4 / 4.0 / 1.7	**19** SU	0538 / 1104 / 1820 / 2341	3.9 / 1.6 / 4.1 / 1.7	
5 SU	0458 / 1023 / 1740 / 2300	3.8 / 1.5 / 4.0 / 1.7	**20** M	0651 / 1214 / 1925	3.8 / 1.7 / 4.0	
6 M	0602 / 1130 / 1842	3.8 / 1.6 / 4.0	**21** TU	0052 / 0805 / 1323 / 2026	1.7 / 3.8 / 1.8 / 4.0	
7 TU	0009 / 0712 / 1239 / 1947	1.6 / 3.9 / 1.5 / 4.2	**22** W	0157 / 0910 / 1423 / 2121	1.6 / 3.9 / 1.7 / 4.1	
8 W	0116 / 0821 / 1345 / 2051	1.4 / 4.1 / 1.4 / 4.3	**23** TH	0250 / 1003 / 1512 / 2210	1.5 / 4.0 / 1.6 / 4.1	
9 TH	0218 / 0927 / 1447 / 2151	1.2 / 4.3 / 1.2 / 4.5	**24** F	0336 / 1047 / 1555 / 2252	1.3 / 4.2 / 1.4 / 4.2	
10 F	0317 / 1027 / 1543 / 2247	1.0 / 4.4 / 1.0 / 4.6	**25** SA	0415 / 1125 / 1632 / ● 2329	1.2 / 4.3 / 1.3 / 4.3	
11 SA	0411 / 1123 / 1636 / O 2339	0.8 / 4.6 / 0.9 / 4.6	**26** SU	0450 / 1200 / 1708	1.1 / 4.3 / 1.2	

AUGUST

Day	TIME	M		TIME	M	Day
1 SA	0251 / 0806 / 1525 / 2027	4.1 / 1.0 / 4.3 / 1.3	**16** SU	0356 / 0919 / 1630 / 2147	4.2 / 1.4 / 4.3 / 1.6	
2 SU	0330 / 0847 / 1604 / 2112	4.1 / 1.2 / 4.2 / 1.5	**17** M	0452 / 1017 / 1727 / 2254	3.9 / 1.8 / 4.0 / 1.8	
3 M	0416 / 0937 / 1653 / 2211	3.9 / 1.5 / 4.0 / 1.6	**18** TU	0607 / 1133 / 1838	3.7 / 2.1 / 3.8	
4 TU	0518 / 1045 / 1800 / 2328	3.8 / 1.7 / 3.9 / 1.7	**19** W	0017 / 0737 / 1259 / 1958	2.0 / 3.6 / 2.1 / 3.7	
5 W	0640 / 1210 / 1917	3.8 / 1.8 / 4.0	**20** TH	0138 / 0854 / 1411 / 2106	1.9 / 3.7 / 1.9 / 3.8	
6 TH	0052 / 0806 / 1331 / 2034	1.6 / 3.9 / 1.6 / 4.1	**21** F	0239 / 0951 / 1503 / 2158	1.7 / 3.9 / 1.7 / 4.0	
7 F	0208 / 0919 / 1439 / 2140	1.4 / 4.1 / 1.3 / 4.3	**22** SA	0325 / 1033 / 1544 / 2239	1.4 / 4.1 / 1.4 / 4.2	
8 SA	0311 / 1021 / 1538 / 2239	1.0 / 4.4 / 1.1 / 4.5	**23** SU	0400 / 1106 / 1618 / 2312	1.2 / 4.3 / 1.3 / 4.3	
9 SU	0406 / 1115 / 1629 / O 2329	0.8 / 4.6 / 0.9 / 4.6	**24** M	0432 / 1136 / 1649 / ● 2343	1.0 / 4.4 / 1.1 / 4.3	
10 M	0454 / 1205 / 1717	0.6 / 4.8 / 0.8	**25** TU	0502 / 1205 / 1721	0.9 / 4.4 / 1.0	
11 TU	0015 / 0540 / 1251 / 1802	4.7 / 0.5 / 4.9 / 0.8	**26** W	0011 / 0534 / 1236 / 1753	4.3 / 0.8 / 4.5 / 1.0	

Extract 4

TIDAL DIFFERENCES ON PORTSMOUTH

PLACE	MHW		MLW		GUIDING DEPTH AT			
	Tm. Diff.	Ht. Diff.	Tm. Diff.	Ht. Diff.	HWS	HWN	CD	
	h. min.	m.	h. min.	m.	m.	m.	m.	POSITION
Swanage	− 2 50S − 5 30N	− 2.4	− 1 05	− 0.5	4.5	4.1	2.5	Pierhead
Bournemouth	− 2 40S − 5 00N	− 2.4	− 0 40	− 0.5	4.1	3.7	2.1	Pierhead
Christchurch	− 2 30S + 0 30N	− 2.6	− 0 35	− 0.7	0.8	0.4	− 1.0	Bar (changeable)
Isle of Wight Freshwater Bay	+ 2 05S + 0 15N	− 2.1S − 1.5N	− 0 50	− 0.3	3.6	3.3	1.0	Off Hotel
St. Catherines Pt.	− 0 35	− 0.9	− 0 35	− 0.1	−	−	−	
Ventnor	− 0 25	− 0.7	− 0 25	0.0	6.7	6.0	2.8	Pier head
Sandown	+ 0 00	− 0.5	+ 0 15	− 0.1	5.3	4.5	1.2	Pier head
Bembridge (Brading)	− 0 00	− 1.5	+ 0 10	− 1.0	3.7	2.9	0.6	Bar
Ryde	0 00	− 0.1	− 0 05	0.0	6.5	5.7	2.0	Pier
Wootton Creek ..	− 0 05	− 0.2	− 0 10	0.0	6.8	6.0	2.4	Dredged channel
Cowes	− 0 15S + 0 15N	− 0.4	− 0 10	0.0	7.4	6.7	3.2	Entce. to River Medina
Newport	−	− 0.5	−	+ 0.7	2.3	1.6	− 1.8	
Newtown Creek	− 0 50S + 0 10N	− 1.1	− 0 15	− 0.1	4.3	3.7	0.7	Off Entce. to Creek
Yarmouth	− 1 05S + 0 05N	− 1.4	− 0 25	− 0.2	5.0	4.4	1.9	Castle Pier
Totland Bay	− 1 30S − 0 45N	− 1.8	− 0 40	− 0.3	4.3	3.9	1.6	Pier head
Alum Bay	− 1 40S − 0 50N	− 1.8	− 0 40	− 0.3	−	−	−	Anchorage prohibited
The Solent Hurst Point	− 1 15S − 0 05N	− 1.7	− 0 25	− 0.3	10.7	10.3	8.0	Hurst Road
Keyhaven	− 1 05S 0 00N	− 1.6	− 0 25	− 0.3	6.6	6.1	3.7	In Lake behind bar
Lymington	− 0 55S + 0 05N	− 1.5	− 0 20	− 0.3	4.4	4.0	1.4	Bar
Beaulieu River ...	− 0 25S + 0 05N	− 0.6	− 0 15	− 0.1	4.6	3.8	0.6	Bar

Extract 5

TO FIND DISTANCE OFF LIGHTS RISING OR DIPPING

Height of Light		HEIGHT OF EYE												
		Metres											
		1.5	3	4.6	6.1	7.6	9.1	10.7	12.2	13.7	15.2	16.8	18.3	19.8
		Feet											
		5	10	15	20	25	30	35	40	45	50	55	60	65
m	ft													
12	40	9¾	11	11¾	12½	13	13½	14	14½	15	15½	15¾	16¼	16½
15	50	10¾	11¾	12½	13¼	14	14½	15	15½	15¾	16¼	16¾	17	17½
18	60	11½	12½	13½	14	14¾	15¼	15¾	16¼	16½	17	17½	17¾	18¼
21	70	12¼	13¼	14	14¾	15½	16	16½	17	17¼	17¾	18	18½	19
24	80	13	14	14¾	15½	16	16½	17	17½	18	18½	18¾	19¼	19½
27	90	13½	14½	15½	16	16¾	17¼	17¾	18¼	18½	19	19½	19¾	20¼
30	100	14	15	16	16½	17¼	17¾	18¼	18¾	19¼	19½	20	20½	20¾
34	110	14½	15¾	16½	17¼	17¾	18¼	19	19¼	19¾	20¼	20½	21	21¼
37	120	15¼	16¼	17	17¾	18¼	19	19½	20	20¼	20¾	21	21½	22
40	130	15¾	16¾	17½	18¼	19	19½	20	20½	20¾	21¼	21½	22	22½
43	140	16¼	17¼	18	18¾	19½	20	20½	21	21¼	21¾	22	22½	23
46	150	16¾	17¾	18½	19¼	19¾	20½	21	21¼	21¾	22¼	22½	23	23¼
49	160	17	18¼	19	19¾	20¼	20¾	21½	21¾	22¼	22¾	23	23½	23¾
52	170	17½	18½	19½	20	20¾	21¼	21¾	22¼	22¾	23	23½	24	24¼

Extract 6

ANVIL POINT 50°35.5'N, 1°57.5'W. Lt. Fl. 10 sec. 24M. vis. 237° to 076°. White Tr. 45m.
Horn(3) 30 sec. shown H24.
PEVERIL LEDGE By. Can. R. Off Peveril Pt.

SWANAGE

Pier Lt. 2 F.R. vert. 3M. White mast with lantern, 6m. on N arm of Pier.

POOLE 50°41'N 1°56'W. Tel: Poole (0202) 685261 (Night: Broadstone 692149)
Pilotage: E.T.A. required 12 h and 2 h in advance.
P/Station: Radio—Cutter cruises near Poole Bar By. when required.
Radio—Port: VHF Chan. 16, 14. Hours 0900-1700 Mon.-Fri.
Radio—Pilots: VHF Chan. 16, 14, 9, 6—Cont.
Poole Hbr. Y.C. Marina (0202) 707321. Chan. M. Apr.-Oct. 0800-1600.
Entry Signals: Floating breakwater of tyres showing 6 in. above water between Fishermans Dock breakwater and centre dolphin opp. Town Quay. Vessels navigating between Little Channel, Fishermans Dock and E end of Town Quay should not pass between centre of E Dolphins and W end of Fishermans Dock breakwater.
Lifting Bridge between Poole Town and Lower Hamworthy.
R.Lt.—do not approach bridge (vessels entitled to request bridge to be opened contact Poole Bridge on VHF Chan. 14.)
Do not pass Stakes Lt. By. until distant signal observed.
Bridge opening times: Mon.-Fri. 0930, 1130, 1430, 1630, 1830, 2130, 2330; Sat.-Sun. & Bank Hol. 0730, 0930, 1130, 1330, 1530, 1730, 1930, 2130.
Sandbanks Ferry when working displays 1 B. ball or W., G., R. Lts. vert. Ferry gives way to other vessels in Harbour. Sound 4 short blasts for ferry to keep clear. Allow enough time for ferry to manoeuvre.

SWASH CHANNEL

POOLE FAIRWAY Lt.By. L.Fl. 10 sec. Pillar R.W.V.S. Topmark Sph. Bell.
TRAINING BANK Lt.Bn. Q.R. 2M. R.Tr. 7m. marks seaward end of training wall on SW side of Swash Channel. 10 stakes with R. Can. Topmarks at intervals along Training Bank.

Bar No: 1 Lt.By. Q.G. Conical G. Bell.	**No: 2 Lt.By.** Fl.(2)R. 10 sec. Can.R.
No: 3 By. Conical G.	No: 4 By. Can R.
No: 5 By. Conical G.	No: 6 Punch & Judy By. Can. R.
No: 7 By. Conical G.	No: 8 By. Can. R.
No: 9 By. Conical G.	No: 10 By. Can. R.
No: 11 By. Conical G.	**No: 12 Channel Lt.By.** Fl.R. 3 sec. Can. R.
HOOK SANDS No: 13 Lt.By. Fl.G. 3 sec.	W of centre inner end Swash Channel.
Conical G.	No: 14 By. Can. R.
HOOK SANDS Bn. B.Y. Topmark N.	No: 16 By. Can. R.
No: 15 By. Conical G.	
No: 17 By. Conical G.	
No: 19 By. Conical G.	

SOUTH HAVEN POINT. Sandbanks Ferry Lts. Q.R. Ferry Landing.
NORTH HAVEN POINT. W of Haven Hotel (Conspicuous).
SAND BANKS. Lt.Bn. F.Or. 10M. vis. 315°-135° 4m. R.C.
FERRY LANDING. Lt. 2 F.G. vert. on W side of Ramp. (When approaching signal 4 long blasts.)

continued

Extract 6 *continued*

EAST LOOE CHANNEL

EAST LOOE Lt.By. Q.R. Can. R. marks E Looe Chan.
EAST HOOK By. Can. R. marks E. side Hook Sands.
EAST LOOE Lt.Bn. Oc.W.R.G. 6 sec. W.10M., R.6M., G.6M. Col. 9m. R.234°-294°; W.294°-304°; G.304°-024°.

N. HAVEN POINT. Lt.Bn. Q.(9) 15 sec. Topmark W.
3 Cable Bns. Lt.F. between N Haven Pt. and Brownsea Castle.
18a Lt.By. Fl.(2)R. 5 sec. Can. R.
No. 18 Lt.By. Fl.R. 5 sec. Can. R.

POOLE TO NEEDLES CHANNEL

POOLE HEAD By. Can. Y. marks sewer off Poole Head.
BRANKSOME CHINE By. Can. Y. marks sewer off Branksome.
ALUM CHINE By. Can. Y. marks pipes off Alum Chine.
WHITBREAD MARK YACHT RACING By. Can.Y.

BOURNEMOUTH 50°43′N, 1°52′W. Tel: Bournemouth 28282.
Entry Signals: R. flag or R. Lt. at Bournemouth or Boscombe Pier at half mast—vessels must not go alongside.

PIER HEAD. 2 F.R. vert. 2m. apart, white post with lantern, 8m. 1M. Reed(2) 120 sec. when ships expected. Also bell to assist steamers.
BOURNEMOUTH PIER OUTFALL. By. Can. Y. marks drain pipes near Pier.

BOSCOMBE 50°43′N, 1°50′W
PIER HEAD. 2 F.R. vert. on R. Col. 7m. 1M. F.R.Lts. on hotel shown 289.5°, 0.51M. from Pier Lt.
BOSCOMBE PIER OUTFALL. By. Can. Y.

CHRISTCHURCH 50°47′N, 1°50′W
Air Lt. Al.Fl.W.G. 10 sec. at Hurn Aerodrome.
CHRISTCHURCH LEDGE By. Pillar Y.B. Topmark S.
CHRISTCHURCH BAY WAVE RESEARCH. Struct.Lt.Bn. Mo(U) 15 sec. Mo(U) R. 15 sec. 8m. Horn Mo(U) 30 sec.
N HEAD. 50°42.6′N, 01°35.4′W Lt.By. Fl.(3)G. 10 sec. Conical G. marks W end N Chan. apprs. to the W Solent.

Extract 7

JULY

G.M.T.   (31 days)   G.M.T.

			Equation of Time		Transit	Semi-diam.	Lat. 52°N.				Lat. Corr. to Sunrise, Sunset, etc.				
	DATE						⊙	SUN	⊙						
Yr.	Mth.	Week	0 h.	12 h.	Transit	Semi-diam.	Twi-light	Sun-rise	Sun-set	Twi-light	Lat.	Twi-light	Sun-rise	Sun-set	Twi-light
	Day of		m. s.	m. s.	h. m.		h. m.	h. m.	h. m.	h. m.	°	h. m.	h. m.	h. m.	h. m.
182	1	W	+03 38	+03 44	12 04	15.8	02 55	03 44	20 23	21 12	N70	S.A.H.	S.A.H.	S.A.H.	S.A.H.
183	2	Th	+03 50	+03 55	12 04	15.8	02 56	03 44	20 23	21 12	68	S.A.H.	S.A.H.	S.A.H.	S.A.H.
184	3	F	+04 01	+04 07	12 04	15.8	02 57	03 45	20 23	21 11	66	T.A.N.	-2 21	+2 19	T.A.N.
185	4	Sa	+04 12	+04 18	12 04	15.8	02 58	03 46	20 22	21 10	64	T.A.N.	-1 42	+1 40	T.A.N.
186	5	Sun	+04 23	+04 28	12 04	15.8	02 59	03 47	20 22	21 10	62	-2 21	-1 14	+1 14	+2 21
187	6	M	+04 34	+04 39	12 05	15.8	03 00	03 48	20 21	21 09	N60	-1 27	-0 54	+0 54	+1 27
188	7	Tu	+04 44	+04 49	12 05	15.8	03 01	03 49	20 20	21 08	58	-0 55	-0 37	+0 37	+0 56
189	8	W	+04 53	+04 58	12 05	15.8	03 03	03 50	20 20	21 07	56	-0 33	-0 22	+0 23	+0 34
190	9	Th	+05 03	+05 07	12 05	15.8	03 04	03 51	20 19	21 06	54	-0 15	-0 10	+0 11	+0 15
191	10	F	+05 12	+05 16	12 05	15.8	03 05	03 52	20 18	21 05	50	+0 13	+0 10	-0 10	-0 13
192	11	Sa	+05 20	+05 24	12 05	15.8	03 07	03 53	20 18	21 04	N45	+0 39	+0 30	-0 30	-0 39
193	12	Sun	+05 28	+05 32	12 06	15.8	03 08	03 54	20 17	21 03	40	+0 59	+0 46	-0 46	-0 59
194	13	M	+05 36	+05 39	12 06	15.8	03 09	03 55	20 16	21 02	35	+1 16	+1 00	-0 59	-1 16
195	14	Tu	+05 43	+05 46	12 06	15.8	03 11	03 56	20 15	21 00	30	+1 30	+1 12	-1 11	-1 30
196	15	W	+05 50	+05 53	12 06	15.8	03 12	03 57	20 14	20 59	20	+1 53	+1 32	-1 31	-1 52
197	16	Th	+05 56	+05 59	12 06	15.8	03 13	03 58	20 13	20 58	N10	+2 12	+1 46	-1 48	-2 11
198	17	F	+06 02	+06 04	12 06	15.8	03 15	04 00	20 12	20 56	0	+2 28	+2 05	-2 04	-2 27
199	18	Sa	+06 07	+06 09	12 06	15.8	03 16	04 01	20 11	20 55	S10	+2 43	+2 21	-2 19	-2 43
200	19	Sun	+06 12	+06 14	12 06	15.8	03 17	04 02	20 10	20 54	20	+2 59	+2 38	-2 36	-2 59
201	20	M	+06 16	+06 18	12 06	15.8	03 19	04 04	20 08	20 52	30	+3 15	+2 57	-2 54	-3 15
202	21	Tu	+06 19	+06 21	12 06	15.8	03 20	04 05	20 07	20 51	S35	+3 25	+3 08	-3 06	-3 25
203	22	W	+06 23	+06 24	12 06	15.8	03 22	04 06	20 06	20 50	40	+3 35	+3 21	-3 18	-3 35
204	23	Th	+06 25	+06 26	12 06	15.8	03 24	04 08	20 04	20 48	45	+3 38	+3 36	-3 33	-3 47
205	24	F	+06 27	+06 28	12 06	15.8	03 25	04 09	20 03	20 46	S50	+4 02	+3 55	-3 51	-4 02
206	25	Sa	+06 29	+06 29	12 06	15.8	03 27	04 10	20 02	20 45					
207	26	Sun	+06 29	+06 30	12 06	15.8	03 29	04 12	20 00	20 43					
208	27	M	+06 30	+06 30	12 06	15.8	03 30	04 13	19 58	20 41					
209	28	Tu	+06 29	+06 29	12 06	15.8	03 32	04 15	19 57	20 40					
210	29	W	+06 28	+06 28	12 06	15.8	03 34	04 17	19 55	20 38					
211	30	Th	+06 27	+06 26	12 06	15.8	03 35	04 18	19 54	20 36					
212	31	F	+06 25	+06 23	12 06	15.8	03 37	04 19	19 53	20 34					

For longitude west, add 4 minutes per degree.
For longitude east, subtract 4 minutes per degree.

Index

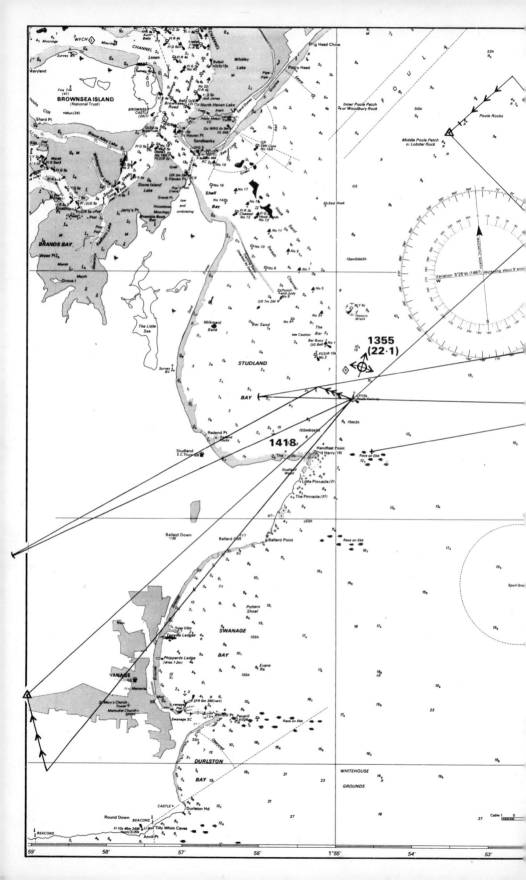